Stunning Stitches
for crazy quilts

480 Embroidered Seam Designs
36 STITCH-TEMPLATE DESIGNS FOR PERFECT PLACEMENT

Kathy Seaman Shaw

C&T PUBLISHING

Text copyright © 2019 by Kathy Seaman Shaw

Photography and artwork copyright © 2019 by C&T Publishing, Inc.

Publisher: Amy Marson

Creative Director: Gailen Runge

Acquisitions Editor: Roxane Cerda

Managing Editor: Liz Aneloski

Editor: Kathryn Patterson

Technical Editor: Linda Johnson

Cover/Book Designer: April Mostek

Production Coordinator: Tim Manibusan

Production Editor: Jennifer Warren

Illustrators: Linda Johnson, Kirstie Pettersen, and Kathy Seaman Shaw

Photo Assistants: Mai Yong Vang and Rachel Holmes

Cover photography by Mai Yong Vang

How-to photography by Kelly Burgoyne and quilt photography by Mai Yong Vang of C&T Publishing, Inc., unless otherwise noted

Published by C&T Publishing, Inc., P.O. Box 1456, Lafayette, CA 94549

Library of Congress Cataloging-in-Publication Data

Names: Shaw, Kathy Seaman, author.

Title: Stunning stitches for crazy quilts : 480 embroidered seam designs, 16 stitch-template designs for perfect placement / Kathy Seaman Shaw.

Description: Lafayette, CA : C&T Publishing, Inc., [2019]

Identifiers: LCCN 2018037407 | ISBN 9781617457739 (softcover : alk. paper)

Subjects: LCSH: Embroidery--Patterns. | Quilting--Patterns. | Crazy quilts.

Classification: LCC TT771 .S5 2019 | DDC 746.44--dc23

LC record available at https://lccn.loc.gov/2018037407

Printed in the USA

10 9 8 7 6 5

Dedication

This book is dedicated to my mom,
who is the constant love in my life.

Acknowledgments

Heartfelt thanks to my family for always being supportive. Love to my darlings, Sommer and Aidan, who keep me moving forward each day. Hugs to all the ladies that stitch with me in the various crazy endeavors I dream up for us to do via the *Shawkl Designs* blog (shawkl.com) and the group sites at Yahoo and Facebook—y'all are just the best cyber friends a gal could have. A special shout-out to my seam-stitching buddies Katie and Cindy Bock—hugs to you both.

A huge thanks to each of the generous companies that provided items used in the stitching of the models and the staging of the photographs for this book:

Andover Fabrics, Inc. (andoverfabrics.com): Cotton fabrics for sampler blocks

Cartwright's Sequins (ccartwright.com): Sequins

Cloud9 Fabrics (cloud9fabrics.com): Tinted denim fabrics for sampler blocks

Clover (clover-usa.com): Hoop, needle, and silk threads

Coats & Clark (makeitcoats.com): Specialty button thread and sewing thread

Colour Complements (etsy.com/shop/colourcomplements): Hand-dyed fibers

Creative Impressions (creativeimpressions.com): Seam templates

The DMC Corporation (dmc.com): Perle cotton #12

Dear Stella (dearstelladesign.com): Cotton fabrics for sampler blocks

Fire Mountain Gems and Beads (firemountaingems.com): Montées, Loch Rosen, and beads

Fiskars (fiskars.com): Rotary cutter, mats, mat board knives, and scissors

June Tailor, Inc. (junetailor.com): Pressing mats and rotary cutter

Just Another Button Company (justanotherbuttoncompany.com): Tiny buttons

Kreinik Mfg. Co., Inc. (kreinik.com): Braids and metallic threads

Pellon (pellonprojects.com): Fusible interfacing

Sulky (sulky.com): Petite thread sampler

YLI (ylicorp.com): Silk sewing thread

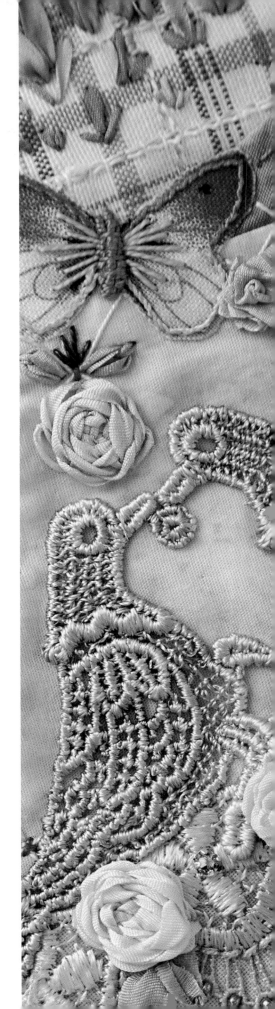

Contents

Preface

My great-grandmother never had idle hands and she loved to quilt. She probably passed down this trait to me; I find this likely, as my grandparents, mother, and sisters do not love to sew. The joy of working with a needle appeared early in my adulthood and has remained constant in my life.

Today, I count my quilting skills in decades. I have spent my adult life so far volunteering my time to teach traditional quilt classes at local quilt shops wherever I've lived. When a cyber friend wanted to swap 6″ Heart blocks in the crazy quilt style, I signed up, even though I had not done a crazy quilt before. Then immediately I began to panic.

My embroidery skills were very basic at best. These first blocks had a lot of trims and beads on them but little stitching. This embarrassing fact made me upset with myself; it felt like a failure. The problem was that I was also a workingwoman with a position as an analyst in the military requiring a lot of travel. So I really had no time to learn a lot of new embroidery stitches and crazy quilting during this time frame.

This got me thinking. How many crazy quilt seams could I create with just the few basic stitches I already knew? I began journaling seam ideas and soon had several pages filled with these basic seam designs. This blossomed into the creation of a personal challenge to stitch a sampler of seams and blog about this process. The "Twelve Dozen in Twelve Months" challenge and my *Shawkl Designs* blog (shawkl.com) were launched. My life was about to really change!

Back then, I created some small templates with graph paper to mark the needle-up and needle-down positions for the first layer of embroidery on my seams. The result was embroidery that was neat and uniformly spaced. That gave me confidence.

Over time, I started teaching free online classes, adult quilting courses at the local college, and regional classes for quilt groups. Basically, I shared with anyone that would listen how wonderful stitch templates were and how much improved my own embroidery had become because of them. So even if your embroidery skills are less than you'd like them to be … don't give up! Consider using the stitch-template designs in this book to make stitch templates that will improve the look of your embroidery.

Students were so enthused with the ease of using templates that my classes expanded to include more techniques like silk ribbon embroidery, dimensional threadwork, and all aspects of crazy quilting. Next, the publication of a book series on crazy quilting was launched with Amazon. This writing journey is now culminated with the book you have in your hands today.

Introduction

Background

A *crazy quilt* is widely viewed as a quilt having a patchwork design that appears more like fractured glass than a traditional uniform setting of blocks and rows. Today, crazy quilts are heavily embellished on top of this fabric patchwork layer, but early crazy quilts included only thread embroidery work. In the early 1900s, crazy quilts included some embroidery within the fabric patches as well as along the seamlines. In the mid-1900s, magazines began including embroidery motif patterns to encourage readers to embellish the fabric patch area between seams, advertising the beautiful and affordable new silk threads. Still, seams themselves remained relatively simple in color and design, using only different types of thread. Lace or cording was more often promoted as embellishment for home or garment items, so these early quilts included primarily embroidery stitching.

Opulent silk or velvet fabrics were often seen in the construction of small lap-size quilts, with embellished seams of delicate embroidery stitches. The fabrics were just as important as the embroidery work and were often garment remnants from women's dresses or men's waistcoats. Less affluent

seamstresses would use common fabrics in their crazy quilts, surely desiring to be part of the "crazy" phenomena as best as they could afford. The fancy-fabric quilts were displayed across furniture in the parlor room, where visiting guests were often entertained. This gave the mistress of the house a perfect place to showcase her embroidery talents and the wealth of the family based on the opulent fabrics in her crazy quilt.

Lace was rarely included in crazy quilts in early years. Lace was handmade during this time frame and was most likely considered too tedious and time consuming to include in quilts. Then, during the Industrial Revolution era, fabrics, laces, and ribbons became available to women of all economic levels. Quilts began to incorporate other sewn items and crafts of the time period, including hand painting or stamping on velvet, delicate tatting and lace pieces, and the addition of crewel embroidery or silk thread embroidery. Quilts also began to include themes of the time period, such as the inclusion of flowers and romantic symbols or political and social messages, with the addition of sewn-in items like campaign ribbons or political slogans.

During the twentieth century, crazy quilting was influenced by the surge of art quilts into the traditional world of quilting. Art quilts made it acceptable to add various sequins, beads, jewelry components, punched metal pieces, and odd embellishments to a quilt. Modern crazy quilts can include unique and creative embellishing techniques and supplies rather than adhering only to the standard Victorian-style crazy quilt, in which mostly lace and embroidery stitches were used with minimal beads, buttons, appliqué, or silk ribbon embroidery.

Modern crazy quilts continue to have the fractured-glass aspect to them, regardless of their layout or design. Blocks often tell a story or follow a specific theme; this is especially helpful when working on a group round-robin quilt or swapping crazy quilt blocks.

Today, any object that can be sewn in place is acceptable to consider for embellishing crazy quilts. As you might imagine, this results in a very large and diverse collection of embellishment supplies. Crazy quilters search out local secondhand, thrift, hobby, needlework, and garment-sewing establishments—as well as local quilt shops—to find supplies. This hunt can result in the identification of some interesting objects for crazy quilt use. Items can also be interpreted as something else based on their shape and color. For example, a lace motif can be combined with couched fibers to create a tree shape.

The seam designs in this book include buttons, beads, sequins, silk, and fibers. But don't let the fact that the illustrated designs include mostly round beads or sequins hamper your creativity. Each of these seam designs is flexible so that elements within can be easily altered or substituted. If you don't have the buttons or beads shown in a seam within your stash of supplies, simply substitute another object.

Using the Book Effectively

This book has three main parts: templates, stitching instructions, and seam-design illustrations.

Creating and Using Stitch Templates (page 19) is an optional section. While it is not mandatory that you use templates, they have certainly improved my own crazy quilting endeavors, so I think they are important. If you prefer to freehand stitch all the designs in this book without the use of templates, that's certainly fine.

It is possible to create your own templates for a moderate cost. The value of creating your own set is that you have the option to rescale the size of the templates and increase your available tools easily. This section includes all the information about how to do this. If using templates is a new concept for you, I encourage you to give these a try. They have truly changed the quality of my own embroidery so much and are so easy to create and use! If you prefer to purchase templates, a set specifically designed to work with this book is available at Creative Impressions (creativeimpressions.com) or at your local quilt shop (through Checker Distributors).

Embroidery Stitches (page 28) is the how-to portion of the book and includes creating individual stitches, starting and ending work, and creating flowers and other motifs shown in the seam designs. Simple thread and ribbon stitches can be combined to create clusters of stitches that resemble flowers, fans, or other objects. Each of these combinations is shown as a unique symbol in the seam designs. Creation of these various elements, with clear full-color diagrams and finished photos, is shown in Creating Flowers (page 40) and Creating Shapes and Objects (page 46).

480 Seam Designs Organized by Base-Seam Stitch Type (page 64) is a catalog of 480 seam-design illustrations. My best advice here is to consider each seam design as a starting point because the weight and color of the fibers used, the types of other embellishments shown, and even the design itself is open to change. Consider your own personal style and alter the seam-design ideas as you desire. The only constraint is your own imagination (and perhaps your supply of embellishments on hand), so don't be deterred. Experiment with the designs, adjust, and keep stitching!

If you are fairly confident in your embroidery skill using threads and silk ribbon, then you'll be able to begin stitching these seam designs right away. The illustrations make it easy to understand how the seam is created in layers of embroidery, embellishing with beads, and so on. The main concept to understand in creating the seam designs is that every seam contains *layers* of embellishing.

Building Layered Seams

Crazy quilt seams often appear complex but are usually easy to create once you understand that each seam is built in layers. While there are multiple layers, not every seam includes all possible layers. When viewing the designs, always look for the base seam used. Whether you use the template identified in the design to mark your stitch placement or freehand stitch this part, the base seam will *always* be stitched first. The base seam is easy to identify in a seam design since it is shown in black ink for each of these designs.

tip The *base seam* is the most critical layer, since all other layers of embellishments are created around and on top of this first layer.

As an example, here is Seam Design 90 (page 76). Let's look at all the layers within this specific design.

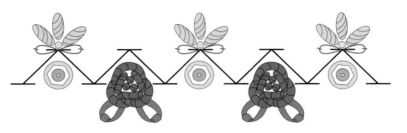

The first layer is the base seam, shown in black. For this specific seam design, the base is a series of Chevron embroidery stitches.

Other designs might use a different base (such as a series of Blanket, Cretan, Feather, Herringbone, or Straight Stitches) rather than this Chevron Stitch base. Also, variety in the width, height, and spacing of stitches can be created even if the basic embroidery stitch type remains the same. So there could be multiple base-seam designs for a series of Chevron embroidery stitches. Each of these variations has a unique stitch-template design (pages 22–27) provided in the book. The designs drawn for a specific variation may even work for other variations, providing endless possibilities for your own creativity in stitching seams.

The next layer of stitching is any additional fiber embroidery work. For Seam Design 90, this is the series of Detached Chain leaves and Bullion Stitch buds along the top of the seam design.

The next layer is any additional silk ribbon or other fiber embroidery. For Seam Design 90, this is the series of ribbon Detached Chain leaves and Bullion Stitch flowers at the base of the seam. Silk ribbon work is done after the fiber work only because it is easy to snag and damage the ribbon. Creating it after the fiber embroidery helps to protect it.

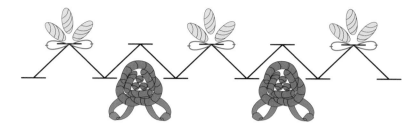

The last layer is always the attachment of any baubles or beads—*everything* snags on these if they are already in place before the embroidery begins. Adding them last eliminates or greatly reduces the frustration of un-snagging fibers and ribbons that get caught on the beads and baubles as the embroidery is worked.

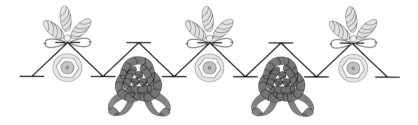

Follow this general layering guide to create all the seam designs in this book. The layering will always begin with the base seam and always end with the baubles and beads. Fiber embroidery is always worked before the silk ribbon, except when the fibers are used as accents, such as French Knots in the center of a flower.

The base seams are not the only simple embroidery stitches used in the designs. Other embroidery stitches accompany the base seam as the layers are added. The designs in this book include more simple embroidery stitches in these layers, including French Knots, Bullion Stitches, and Detached Chain Stitches. Instructions for creating all the thread embroidery stitches are in Combination Embroidery Stitches (page 37).

The silk ribbon embroidery layers have some stitches that seem to be the same whether done in thread or ribbon. But this is not true when you consider the nature of working with ribbon for embroidery. Plus, there are some "new" embroidery stitches in ribbon that don't occur when using thread. Even so, *all* the stitches are considered *very* simple to create.

Consider the individual layers as you view each diagramed seam design. You can distinguish the layers by noting which item is shown below (behind)

another when there are multiple fibers used. One exception to this is the addition of leaves to some flowers. It is easier to lift the edge of a flower to add the leaves rather than trying to weave or manipulate ribbon to create the flower heads on top of existing leaves. This requires that the edge of a flower be lifted or nudged aside with your finger at times as you needle up to begin stitching the leaves. It is easier to nudge existing flower heads aside than to prevent stabbing an existing leaf as the flower head is worked above it.

The last layer is always used to secure any beads, sequins, and so on as part of the seam design. I like using silk thread for sewing on beads and sequins. Silk thread is strong but superthin, so multiple passes through even a tiny bead by needle and thread is possible.

The base template designs (pages 22–27) in the book are provided to help ensure that your completed seam will be neat and uniformly spaced. The templates assist you in marking the specific location of this base seam on your fabric. While each of the seam designs in this book can be freehand stitched without marking on the fabric, it is strongly suggested that all beginner- to intermediate-level embroiderers consider using the templates to create the base-seam layer. Additional motif template designs are included to assist in the spacing of some common elements within the designs, such as the prong grouping (see Prongs, page 48) of Straight Stitches.

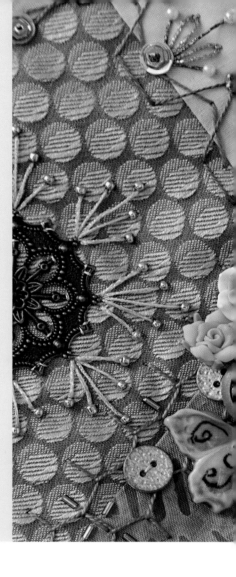

Beginning Embroidery Work

There are differences in how embroidery work should begin and end, depending on whether you use ribbon or thread. Thread fibers can hang loose once a needle is threaded, but silk ribbon should be anchored to the eye of the needle.

Thread-Fiber Embroidery

Crazy quilt blocks are constructed with an extra foundation layer of fabric to accommodate the heavy weight of the embellishing, so it is fine to begin work in thread fibers with a knot. Simply loop the thread around your finger and roll off the finger to form a knot.

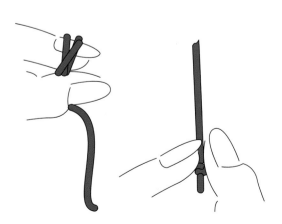

Silk Ribbon Embroidery

Securing the silk ribbon to the eye of the needle will eliminate the need for constant rethreading of the needle.

ANCHOR THE RIBBON TO THE NEEDLE EYE

Begin by threading the ribbon end through the eye of a chenille needle, leaving a short tail about 3″ long. Pierce the end of this short tail about ½″ from the end and pull on the long tail of the ribbon. This will cause the shorter end to slide down to the eye of the needle, securing it snugly against the eye. To *unthread*, slide the anchor knot up the length of the needle and pull the short ½″ tail to remove it.

ANCHOR THE RIBBON TO THE FOUNDATION FABRIC

Begin ribbon embroidery by taking a tiny tack stitch on the foundation fabric (at the reverse or back side), being careful to pierce only the layer of foundation and not the patchwork quilt block. Pull the needle until only a small tail (about ½″) of ribbon remains. Pierce this tail end and push the needle through the ribbon, pulling until a small tack stitch is formed snug against the foundation fabric. Now needle up through all layers of the fabric to begin your first silk ribbon embroidery stitch.

Ending Embroidery Work

End the thread or silk ribbon embroidery work in the same manner. Take the needle to the back of your work. Create a small tack stitch; this will hold the embroidery in place. Take a second tack stitch, and before pulling completely, insert the needle through the stitch loop. Pull to tighten, which will cause the stitch loop to capture the thread or ribbon against the foundation fabric. Tack stitches should always be worked *only* in the fabric foundation layer of your crazy quilt block, not through the top piecing layer of fabric. Trim off the excess thread or ribbon after the tack stitches have been created, leaving a tail about ½″ long on the back.

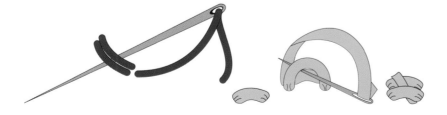

Supplies

This book assumes you already know how to construct a crazy quilt block for embellishment. If you need guidance in this, however, visit *Shawkl Designs* (shawkl.com) for piecing tutorials and free basic crazy quilt courses online.

Embroidery Fibers

Always choose a good-quality cotton floss or perle cotton that is colorfast. The dye colors should not run, even if the project were to get wet. Silk threads are not colorfast, so be careful when using these. It is best to test your fibers before using them in any project that could become wet in the future.

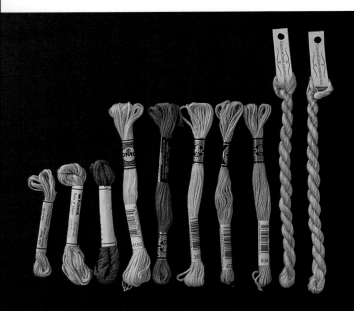

Floss

Standard 6-ply embroidery floss (or 5 ply for silk embroidery threads) works nicely, with 2–3 ply being grouped for the stitching along seams. Once separated, however, the plies will not remain grouped, and therefore the stitching will not be as uniform in appearance as twisted cords or perle produce. Rather, embroidery floss is nice for true thread embroidery motifs but not in seams (in my opinion). If you are adding tiny accents to an object, such as the twisted curl vine on the stem of a pumpkin within a seam, then use a single ply of floss to achieve this tiny detail. Perle would be too bulky in any size to get such a tiny effect. Having a good selection of floss in your stash is still important, even if you choose to use perle for most seam embellishing.

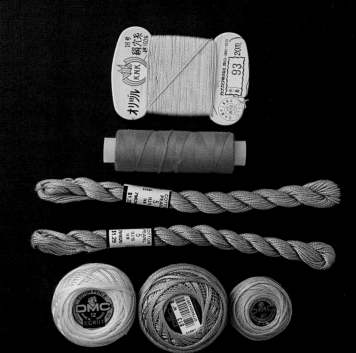

Perle

Threads are machine twisted to form a thin cord that is not easily separated. Perle is most commonly cotton; other fibers (rayon, silk, and so on) may be referred to as *braid* or *cording*. Each is of a uniform size and twist and is used as a single thread rather than working with multiple plies. The thickness of the individual threads will determine the size of the specific twisted cording. Using a variety of sizes and colors within a single seam design can help to create interest by increasing the texture of the seam.

My own personal preference is to use twisted perle cotton for the base-seam designs in this book. Perle cotton comes in sizes 12, 8, 5, and 3. My recommendation is to use size 8 for standard quilt blocks and size 12 if you are creating tiny-scale objects such as pincushions, purses, and the like. Sizes 5 and 3 are so large that they are just too bulky for most seams, but they do work well in extremely large blocks.

Fancy Fibers

Today, there is a large group of fibers that can be used in embellishing. The fancier types include velvet cord, metallic twisted cords, knit soft tubes, and chenille. Several companies combine similar colors of various fiber content to use in embellishing, making it easy on the consumer to obtain a selection that will work well together.

Braids, Cords, Twine, Yarn, and the Like

Even items not specifically marketed for embroidery can be used for some seam work if they can be pulled through fabrics using a chenille or large milliners needle. Some may require a larger needle size and more effort to pull through the fabrics, but they can add nice texture to a project.

Metallic Threads

Metallic fibers are wonderful to include, especially for straight stitches within a seam. The embroidery stitches in these designs are simple and do not require a lot of twisting of the threads, making metallic braids and cording a perfect choice to add sparkle and shine even without the addition of sequins or beads.

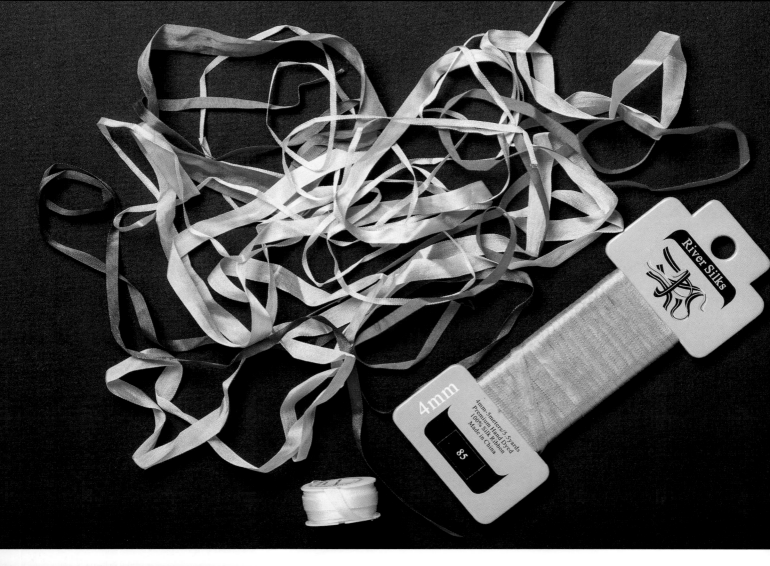

Silk Ribbon

There is really no substitute for silk ribbon. While it can be possible to use satin, rayon, or other types of ribbon for a limited number of flowers, nothing works as nicely as silk for embroidery.

Routinely, silk ribbon for embroidery is limited to 2 mm, 4 mm, 7 mm, and 13 mm widths. The chosen width will depend on the scale of the item you are creating. Seams are more commonly embroidered using the 2 mm width for stitches and the 4 mm, 7 mm, and 13 mm widths for floral motifs. Flowers within the seam designs in this book can be stitched in any size, but 4 mm or 7 mm is the most common size of ribbon to use for Woven Roses, Irises, Tulips, Stem Stitch Roses, and Wrapped Roses. 2 mm or 4 mm is more often used for Detached Chain flowers such as daisies. Leaves are best done in 2 mm or 4 mm if they are Detached Chains or Straight Stitches, while 7 mm is perfect for Ribbon Stitch leaves.

Still, there is no set rule on the size of ribbon to use; it will depend on the scale needed for the specific project and your own personal preference or style.

Needles

There is an almost endless variety of needle types and sizes on the market today. It is important to use the correct style of needle for some tasks, while other tasks can use any type or size with impressive results. Sometimes it can be confusing to choose the right needle. Over time, I have found that my personal preference is to use mostly chenille and milliners needles; this has simplified my stitching life!

Your choice of needle will depend on the size of thread, ribbon, or cording you are working with, as well as your own preferences. Regardless of the type of needle, always choose a size that allows easy passage through the fabric. It is better to use a too-large size than a too-small size. If you find that you are struggling to pull ribbon or thread types through the fabric, change to a larger-size needle.

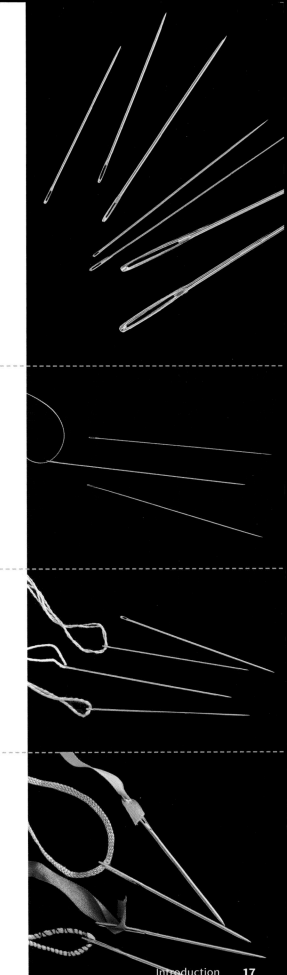

Beading Needles

Beading needles are often used in jewelry making and may be a unique needle to add to your stash. These needles come in short or long lengths, but all are very slender so that they may pass several times through even the tiniest bead. This slender size, however, can create issues when threading. If you find this to be the case, consider changing to a small-size milliners or straw needle. Try several needle types and sizes to find the best one for your chosen beads and your individual eyesight constraints. If beading really is difficult for you, consider a magnification lamp as one of your must-have tools.

Milliners or Straw Needles

These are a must-have for creating knots of any type because the needle shaft is the same thickness from the eye to almost the tip. This lets the coil of wraps around the needle slide along the needle length easily when forming knots. If you have issues getting the thread to pass back through the wraps, most likely you are using a needle that has an eye larger than the shaft size, such as an embroidery needle. Change to a milliners or straw needle to eliminate this problem.

Chenille and Tapestry Needles

Sometimes these are hard to identify in your pincushion, as they look very similar to each other—except for the tip. Chenille needles are very sharp and should always be used for silk ribbon embroidery work. Tapestry needles have dulled round tips; they can be used for weaving ribbon but should not be used for silk ribbon embroidery stitching because it is difficult to pierce the fabric layers with a blunt tip. Since the eye end of a chenille needle works fine to weave ribbon, I don't even include tapestry needles in my stash of crazy quilting supplies. There are several sizes of chenille needles in my pincushion, however, since the size of various cords and ribbons are different.

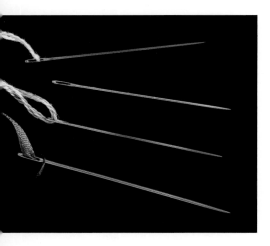

Embroidery Needles

This may be the needle you thought would be used for seam embroidery, but it is designed for ply threads and works best for motifs rather than seams. If you use cording or perle threads, then switch to a large milliners needle. If you prefer working with 6-ply floss, then an embroidery needle remains suitable. These needles have sharp points and long, narrow eyes. An embroidery needle can sometimes be used to work with 2 mm silk ribbon if the fabric layers are not so dense that it is difficult to pierce and pull the ribbon through. The shaft of an embroidery needle is not as strong as that of a chenille needle, so if you do use the embroidery needle and it breaks, change to the chenille needle instead.

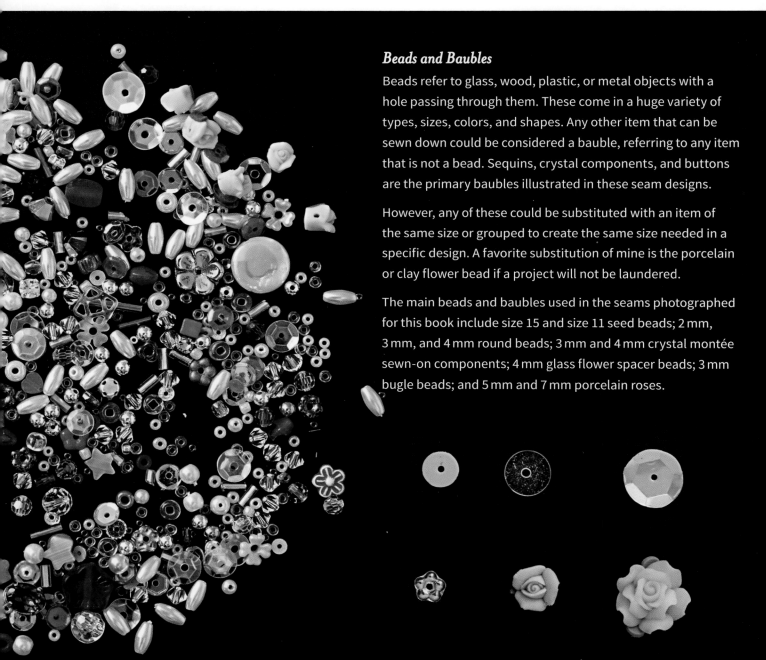

Beads and Baubles

Beads refer to glass, wood, plastic, or metal objects with a hole passing through them. These come in a huge variety of types, sizes, colors, and shapes. Any other item that can be sewn down could be considered a bauble, referring to any item that is not a bead. Sequins, crystal components, and buttons are the primary baubles illustrated in these seam designs.

However, any of these could be substituted with an item of the same size or grouped to create the same size needed in a specific design. A favorite substitution of mine is the porcelain or clay flower bead if a project will not be laundered.

The main beads and baubles used in the seams photographed for this book include size 15 and size 11 seed beads; 2 mm, 3 mm, and 4 mm round beads; 3 mm and 4 mm crystal montée sewn-on components; 4 mm glass flower spacer beads; 3 mm bugle beads; and 5 mm and 7 mm porcelain roses.

Creating and Using Stitch Templates

Stitch templates can be a bit tedious to create, but the time saved after making them is measured in days, not hours. They are so worth the effort! I enjoy using them so much that I now have several different sets of templates created by hand. The very first set I made is still one of my most used. Various sets are handy because they allow the same stitches but in different sizes, scaled to work with small projects (pincushions, purses, scissor cases) or in medium to large projects (tote bags, wallhangings, pillows, and full-size quilt blocks) that I want to create.

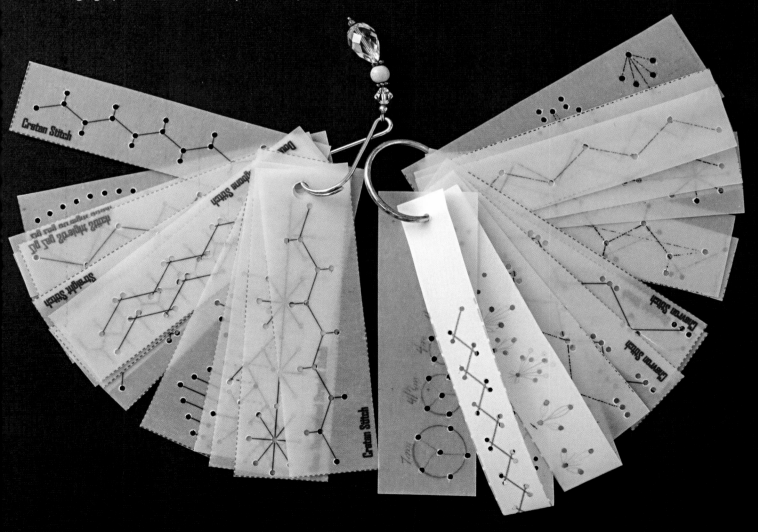

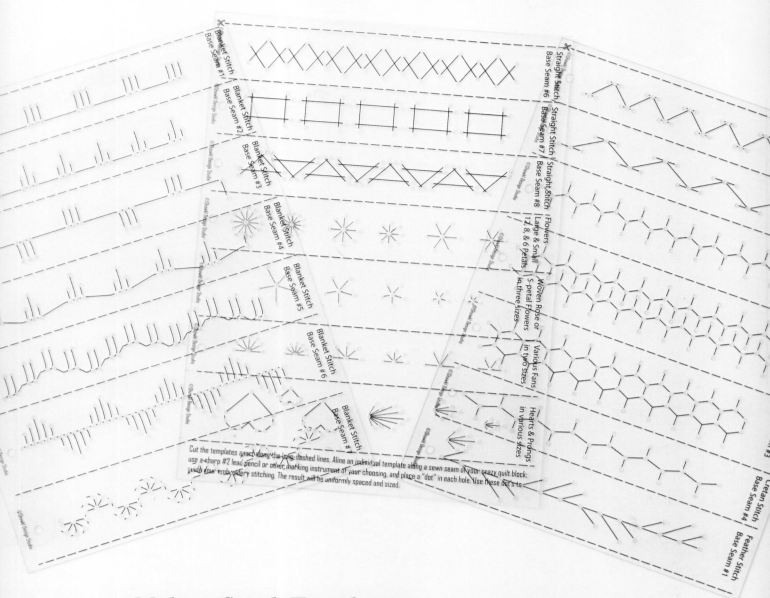

Making Stitch Templates

The templates for this book are available commercially; however, you can also make them yourself. Simply trace or scan the template designs (pages 22–27) and save them as full-size images or pdf pages on your computer. These are scaled for use in 12″–18″ crazy quilt blocks. If you prefer a smaller or larger scale, duplicate the template designs and adjust the percentage on your copier/printer to some amount other than a ratio of 100.

Once the template designs are scanned into a digital file, they can be printed directly to clear or opaque paper. While plastic transparency sheets are an option, they can melt when used in some printers, so I don't recommend using these. Opaque vellum comes in packages of standard-size printer sheets and is opaque enough for templates. Paper does not last quite as long as plastic does, but they do last long enough. Over the past few years, I have created numerous templates for myself to use. While each uses the same simple stitches here in this book, the spacing and scale of each differs with the size of the project I'm working on. There are also shape template designs for individual flower, fan, heart, and prong motifs. I like to keep my templates close when stitching, so they usually are stored in a coffee cup on my desk.

My favorite vellum is Translucent Clear 36 lb Cover by JAM Paper & Envelope (jampaper.com), which is used for covers in presentation packages. It feeds through my inkjet printer with ease and dries quickly. You can also search for 36-pound translucent or opaque vellum on Amazon (amazon.com) or other similar office supply sites. If 36-pound vellum is not available, it is possible to use a lesser weight (the lower the number, the thinner the vellum), but don't go with anything less than 26 pounds for satisfactory results. Do not use a weight higher than 36 pounds, either, as the vellum may not feed through the printer correctly.

Alternately, if you don't have scan capability on your printer, trace the template designs directly to vellum using a fine-point permanent pen. Be careful to let each mark dry completely so you don't smudge the results as you work.

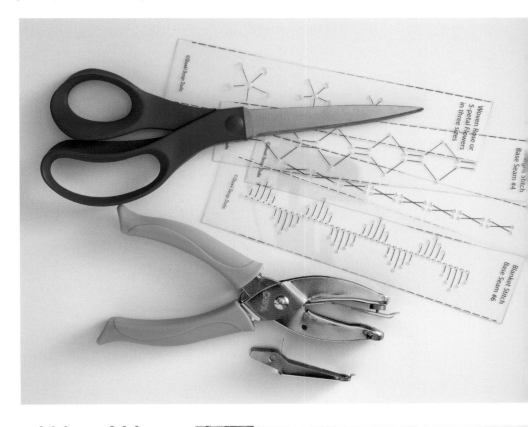

Cut each template apart from the full page of templates along the dotted lines as indicated. Each of the individual stitch templates has small dots to indicate where the needle-up/down position is for that specific embroidery stitch. These dots need to be punched out so that your marking tool can fit inside this hole. Use a tiny hand-held hole punch (1⁄16″ size) to punch out each dot when creating your own templates.

If you do not have a hole punch, you can alternately use a large chenille needle to create the holes. However, a needle will leave rough chads on the back side of the template; remember to put the smooth side of the template against your fabric when marking.

tip Remove the waste-catch attachment from the hole punch so you can see the holes to be punched by flipping the hand-held punch over and viewing from the bottom. When you see the "dot" in the center of the opening, punch it out.

tip It is handy to use a standard-size hole punch to place a hole at the end (about 1⁄2″ inside the edge) of each individual template and then hang them from a ring or length of ribbon. This keeps them organized.

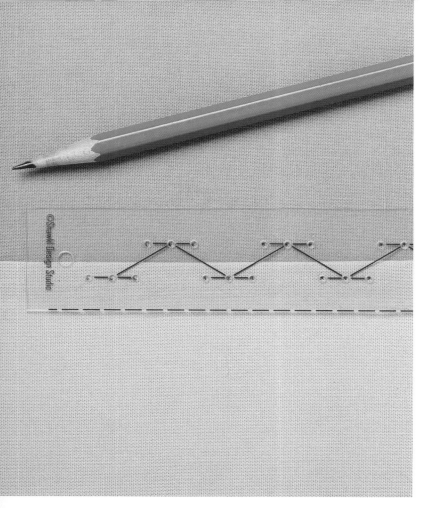

Using Stitch Templates

The template's position on the sewn seam of the fabric block will determine if the embroidery is centered on this seam or positioned slightly above or below it. The decision to center or not depends on the amount of fabric in the patches joined by the sewn seam. Where one patch is significantly larger than the other, it can be advantageous to position the base-seam template over more of that excessive fabric side rather than centering along the sewn seam. Don't worry—the combination stitches will cover the sewn seam area even if the template has been aligned above or below the sewn seam.

The embroidery can begin after the base seam is marked using the template. Marking may require that you move the template along the seamline if the seam is longer than the template. Line up the template carefully before marking any dots on your fabric. Then use a sharp #2 lead pencil (or marking tool of your choice) to place a small dot inside of each punched-out hole in the template. I find that placing the pencil into the hole and then twisting it makes a mark easily.

Use the individual stitch instructions (see Embroidery Stitches, page 28) and the dot markings on the fabric to guide you in the placement of your needle. The instructions will help you to create the specific embroidery stitch by showing you which dot is the next dot to pierce with your needle in the completion of the stitch. Repeat the stitches until you reach the end of the seamline. Secure your thread to the back of the block.

Follow the layering guidelines and stitch instructions to embroider using other threads and complete the designs.

Templates for Base Seams

Template designs are provided (next page and pages 24–27). These can be scanned directly from the book and printed. This complete set of templates can also be purchased at Creative Impressions (creativeimpressions.com).

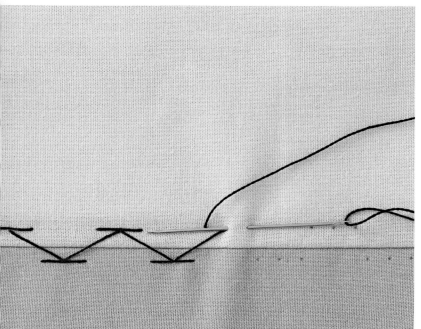

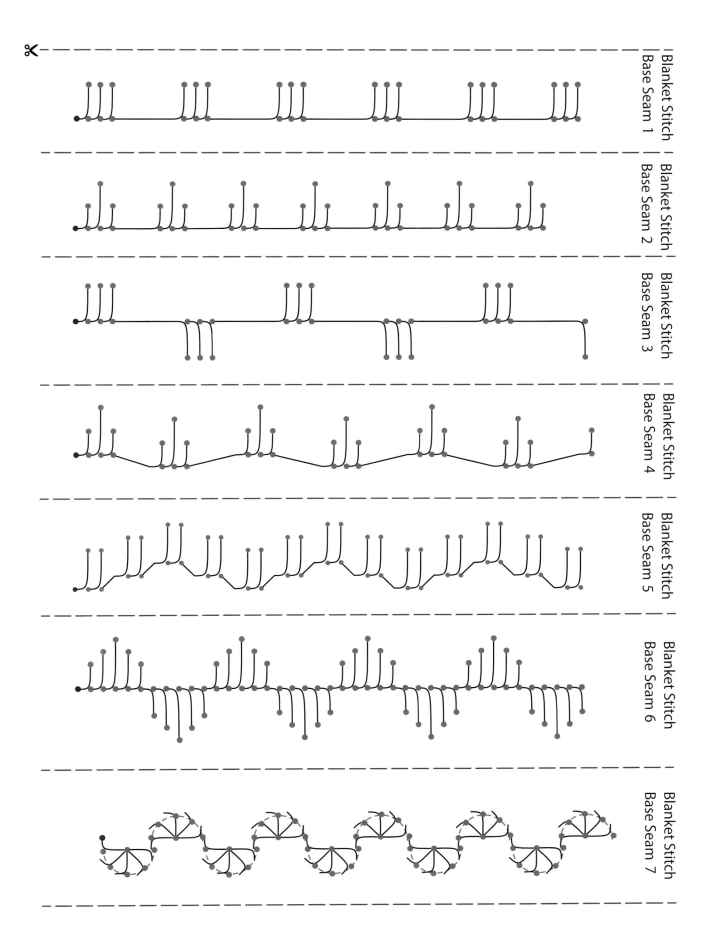

Blanket Stitch Base Seam 1

Blanket Stitch Base Seam 2

Blanket Stitch Base Seam 3

Blanket Stitch Base Seam 4

Blanket Stitch Base Seam 5

Blanket Stitch Base Seam 6

Blanket Stitch Base Seam 7

Feather Stitch Base Seam 2

Feather Stitch Base Seam 3

Feather Stitch Base Seam 4

Feather Stitch Base Seam 5

Herringbone Stitch Base Seam 1

Herringbone Stitch Base Seam 2

Herringbone Stitch Base Seam 3

Herringbone Stitch Base Seam 4

Herringbone Stitch Base Seam 5

Herringbone Stitch Base Seam 6

Straight Stitch Base Seam 1

Straight Stitch Base Seam 2

Straight Stitch Base Seam 3

Straight Stitch Base Seam 4

Straight Stitch Base Seam 5

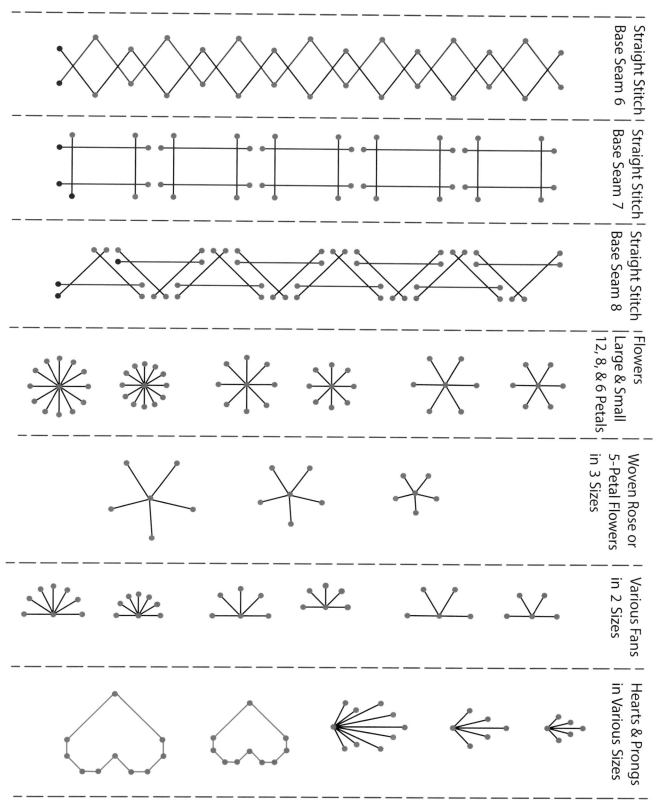

Straight Stitch Base Seam 6

Straight Stitch Base Seam 7

Straight Stitch Base Seam 8

Flowers Large & Small 12, 8, & 6 Petals

Woven Rose or 5-Petal Flowers in 3 Sizes

Various Fans in 2 Sizes

Hearts & Prongs in Various Sizes

Scan, save, and print template pages on clear plastic or opaque vellum. Punch out the red dots, using a 1/16″ hand-held hole punch.

Embroidery Stitches

All of the seam designs in this book use *very* simple embroidery stitches. Each seam involves multiple layers; the first layer is always the *base seam* (shown in black ink on all design charts). The embroidery stitches used for the base seams include the following:

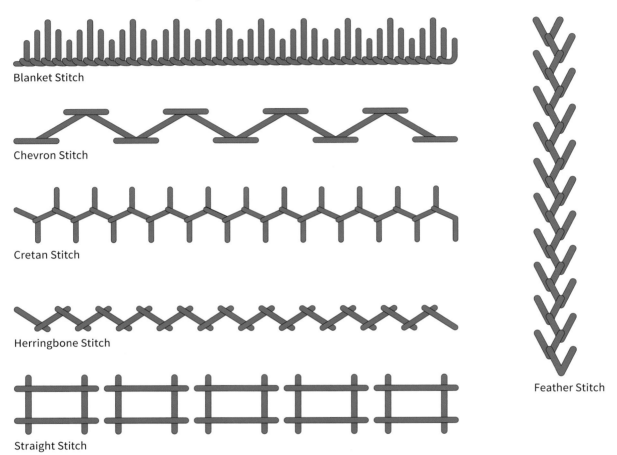

Blanket Stitch

Chevron Stitch

Cretan Stitch

Herringbone Stitch

Straight Stitch

Feather Stitch

Variations of each base seam can be created by changing the size or spacing of the stitches within the seam. The template designs in the previous chapter include all variations shown in the following seam-design charts. The actual creation of each embroidery stitch within a variation is the same; just the spacing or height changes. Let's look at each of these variations and study how the individual stitches are created for each.

color-coded sequences Some of the stitch variations you are about to see require more than one pass to complete. Whenever this is the case, follow the color-coded stitching in this order: red, green, blue, and orange. The corresponding colored letters will show you where the next line of stitching begins. Study the example.

Base-Seam Embroidery Stitches

All the embroidery stitches used to create the base seams are simple to stitch. If you are using the templates, mark the individual base seam following the instructions in Creating and Using Stitch Templates (page 19) first. Then use the following instructions to stitch the base seam using the dots you previously marked to guide your needle placement. *Note:* These embroidery instructions are written for *right-handed* individuals; lefties will need to keep that in mind and adjust to fit left-handed motions. All stitches can be created using a variety of fibers (floss, cording, ribbon, and so on), but the illustrations in this book are using perle cotton for the base-seam embroidery.

Blanket Stitch

Needle up through the **A** dot to begin a line of stitching. Needle down through **B** and up at **C** while keeping your working thread below the needle. Repeat **B** and **C** until you reach the end of your seamline. In sewing, this is called a *Blanket Stitch*.

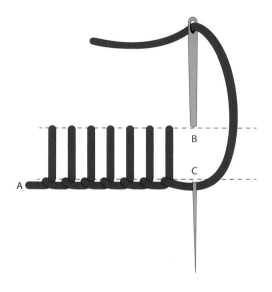

Blanket Stitch Design Variation 1

The height of these Blanket Stitches remains the same across the entire length of the seam; the base of each stitch is level along the seamline. Stitches are grouped into clusters of 3, with the last of the 3 spaced further apart from the next cluster.

Blanket Stitch Design Variation 2

The height of these Blanket Stitches varies, with the center stitch being higher than the stitches on either side of the center. The base of each stitch is level along the seamline. Group Blanket Stitches into uniformly spaced clusters of 3 stitches each. Include additional space between the last of the trio and first of the next trio of stitches.

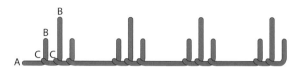

Blanket Stitch Design Variation 3

The height of these Blanket Stitches remains the same across the entire length of the seam; the base of each stitch is level along the seamline. Stitches are grouped into clusters of 3, with the last of the 3 spaced further apart from the next cluster. However, the orientation of each alternate cluster changes, as some are stitched above the seamline and others are stitched below the seamline.

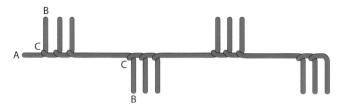

Blanket Stitch Design Variation 4

The height of these Blanket Stitches varies across the entire length of the seam, and the base of each stitch alternates from level along the seamline to slightly below the seamline. Stitches are grouped into clusters of 3, with the last of the 3 spaced further apart from the next cluster.

Blanket Stitch Design Variation 5

The height of these Blanket Stitches is the same across the entire length of the seam. The base of each stitch changes from level along the seamline to above or below the seamline, creating a wavy effect. Stitches are grouped into clusters of 2, with each cluster being spaced equally apart from the previous cluster.

Blanket Stitch Design Variation 6

The height of these Blanket Stitches changes from short to medium to tall to medium to short, creating a cluster of stitches in an angled shape. The group of 5 stitches is aligned along the entire length of the seam so that the base of each stitch is level with the seamline. Stitches are grouped into clusters of 5, with each cluster spaced evenly along the seamline but alternating their direction above or below the seamline.

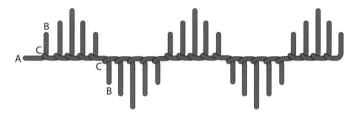

Blanket Stitch Design Variation 7

The height of these Blanket Stitches is the same across the entire length of the seam, but each group of 5 stitches uses the same needle-down hole. The center of each cluster of 5 alternates between sitting slightly above or below the seamline to accommodate the position of the Blanket Stitches. Stitches are grouped into clusters of 5, with all clusters spaced equally apart from the next cluster.

Chevron Stitch

Needle up through the **A** dot to begin stitching. Needle down through **B**, up at **C**, and then down at **D**. Repeat these steps until the line of Chevron Stitches fills the seamline.

Chevron Stitch Design Variation 1

The height of these Chevron Stitches is the same across the entire length of the seam, and the width of each peak/valley is similar in distance to the height of each stitch.

Chevron Stitch Design Variation 2

The height of these Chevron Stitches is the same across the entire length of the seam, but the width of each peak/valley is greater than the height of each stitch.

Cretan Stitch

Cretan Stitching may require you to rotate the hoop so that the seam is in a vertical position rather than horizontal. The stitching is then easily done from top to bottom along 4 imaginary lines. The outer lines are the needle-down positions, and the centerlines are the needle-up positions. The direction of the needle always points the tip towards the center, and the thread always remains below the needle. Needle up at **A**, down at **B**, and up at **C**. Alternate the needle position: left side, right side. Needle down at **B** and up at **C**. Repeat these alternating positions.

Cretan Stitch Design Variation 1

The height of the stitch is the same across the entire length of the seam, and the width of each peak/valley is evenly spaced. The distance between each outer line of needle positions can change to space the stitches close or far apart. Groups of similarly spaced stitches can be aligned to form repeat shapes. (Refer to Color-Coded Sequences, page 28, for help with the multicolored illustrations.)

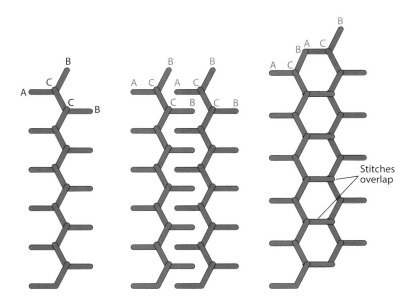

Cretan Stitch Design Variation 2

The height of the stitch is the same across the entire length of the seam, but the width of each peak/valley is greater than the height of each stitch.

Feather Stitch

Feather Stitching may require you to rotate the embroidery hoop so your work is vertical. Individual stitches are created to the left, center, or right of the seamline as you work from top to bottom. Needle up at **A** to begin stitching. Move the needle to the left/right of this position and needle down at **B** and then up at **C**, keeping your thread below the needle. Repeat. Many variations can be created using the Feather Stitch simply by altering the width and depth of each stitch.

Feather Stitch Design Variation 1

The **B** position of this variation is on the seamline, while the **A** and **C** positions are to the right or left of that seamline. Cluster 3 stitches, making the center of the trio longer than the other 2.

Feather Stitch Design Variation 2

The **B** and **C** positions of these Feather Stitches alternate from left to right of the seamline. Uniformly space the **A** and **B** positions level with each other and ensure that the **C** position is the same height continuously.

Feather Stitch Design Variation 3

These Feather Stitches are similar in size and space as the above variations but are grouped to repeat to the left or right. The number of left steps or right steps is consistent to repeat along the seam. This variation is often referred to as a *Double* or *Triple Feather Stitch*, depending on the number of directional steps taken. The stitches have uniform spacing and height in this design variation.

Feather Stitch Design Variation 4

The **B** and **C** positions of these Feather Stitches remain along the seamline. The height of each stitch is longer than the width of each stitch.

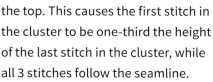

Feather Stitch Design Variation 5

Cluster 3 uniformly spaced stitches to the left or right so that each stitch has the outer side aligned along the top. This causes the first stitch in the cluster to be one-third the height of the last stitch in the cluster, while all 3 stitches follow the seamline.

Herringbone Stitch

Needle up at **A** to begin stitching. Needle down at **B**, up at **C**, down at **D**, and up at **E**. Repeat until you reach the end of your seamline.

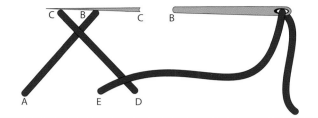

Herringbone Stitch Variation 1

The height of each stitch is the same across the entire length of the seam and the width is equal to the height.

Herringbone Stitch Variation 2

The height of each stitch is the same across the entire length of the seam and the width is about the same as the height, but both are more than that of Variation 2.

Herringbone Stitch Design Variation 3

The stitch height alternates between short and tall, but the base of each is consistently aligned along the seam.

Herringbone Stitch Design Variation 4

The stitch height alternates from tall to short in clusters of 3: 1 tall stitch and 2 short stitches. The base of each stitch is aligned along the seamline.

Herringbone Stitch Design Variation 5

The stitch height alternates from short to tall, but the base of each stitch changes from above or below the seamline.

Herringbone Stitch Design Variation 6

Stitch 2 separate lines of Herringbone Stitches for this variation; both are of uniform height and spacing. Create the first line of stitches, shown in red; the second line of green stitches is layered on top. This repeat creates the illusion of small and large stitches. (Refer to Color-Coded Sequences, page 28, for help with the multicolored illustrations.)

Straight Stitch

Straight stitching is simply needling up at **A** and down at **B**. Repeat as each seam variety diagram indicates until you reach the end of your seamline. Some seam designs will require you to skip over previous Straight Stitches and create these on the return trip, like you might for Cross-Stitching or blackwork pattern embroidery. (Refer to Color-Coded Sequences, page 28, for help with the multicolored illustrations.)

Straight Stitch Design Variation 1

This design variation is a series of angled Straight Stitches, where the peak and valley of each angled stitch moves the needle over horizontally to begin the next angled stitch. This will create space between the angled stitches and leave a series of horizontal stitches on the back of the foundation fabric. Alternate the angle of the individual stitches to complete 1 single row of stitches (shown in red). Repeat the series of stitches, crossing each angle stitch over the previous row of stitches (shown in green).

Straight Stitch Design Variation 2

Here is a simple Straight Stitch, with each right-angle stitch created first by stitching from base to tip and from left to right (shown in red). Then a similar Running Stitch is created from base to tip but stitched from right to left while meeting the prior stitches at the peak and valley of the grouping of stitches (shown in green).

Straight Stitch Design Variation 3

Alternate 1 or 2 angled stitches with a horizontal stitch. Create a series of stitches (shown in red) in a left-to-right direction and then a series of right-to-left stitches (shown in green) to form a continuous line of single stitches. Secondly, repeat another continuous line of stitches (shown in blue and orange), but place the horizontal stitches of this second line slightly below the horizontal stitches of the first line.

Straight Stitch Design Variation 4

This variation is like the above variety, except the position of the second series is placed with the horizontal stitch above the prior line of stitches.

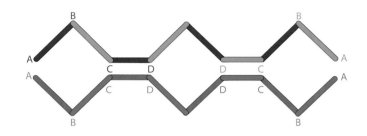

Straight Stitch Design Variation 5

This variation is a series of horizontal and angled vertical stitches. Create the first row (shown in red/green); then layer the second row (shown in blue/orange) on top. Keep the short and tall peaks aligned horizontally.

Straight Stitch Design Variation 6

Create 2 layers of Variation 2, spacing them slightly apart from each other horizontally to create the illusion of small and large diamond shapes.

Straight Stitch Design Variation 7

2 rows of horizontal Straight Stitches (shown in red and green) are layered with a row of tall vertical stitches (shown in blue) so that an open corner-box shape is formed.

Straight Stitch Design Variation 8

A trio of individual Straight Stitches creates a triangle shape with open corners. The sequence of stitches is needle up at **A**, down at **B**, up at **C**, down at **D**, up at **E**, and down at **F**. Then move over to the next trio and repeat.

Straight Stitch in Ribbon

Needle up at **A** and down at **B**. The ribbon will lie flat if the Straight Stitch is about twice the length of the ribbon width. The longer the Straight Stitch, the more likely the ribbon will be easily manipulated to lie flat against the fabric between the **A** and **B** positions.

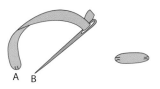

Combination Embroidery Stitches

Additional embroidery stitches layered on top of the base seam are often referred to as *combination stitches*, since these are combined with the basic stitches to create a more elaborate embroidered seam design. While these stitches are usually freehand stitched, some template designs are provided for the more common repeat groups of Straight Stitches to form prongs, fans, circles, and hearts. Marking the placement of these groups of stitches will help to keep them uniformly spaced and of the same size across a seam design.

While combination stitches can be created using any type of fiber, the seam designs in this book use perle cotton or silk ribbon in the illustrations, depending on which type of fiber is recommended. When you create the seams, more interest can be added to your work by changing the color, weight, or types of thread fibers used. You can also change the color and width of silk ribbon to change the size of a flower or object.

Working with silk ribbon is different than working with thread fibers because of its shape. Thread fibers are usually round, while ribbon is flat. This requires a larger hole for the ribbon to travel through and some manipulation for the ribbon to lie flat again once it has exited the hole. Ribbon can also become difficult to pull through if it is pierced when subsequent stitches are created. Be watchful to keep the prior ribbon stitches away from the back of a specific hole you are presently stitching through as you create silk ribbon embroidery stitches.

Back Stitch

Needle up at **A** to begin stitching. Then needle down at **B** and up at **C**. The distance between **A** and **B** should be equal to the distance between **A** and **C**. Repeat to create a line of stitches having no spaces between them.

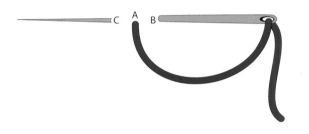

Bullion Stitch

A Bullion Stitch is a type of knot formed by wrapping the thread around the needle multiple times; the number of wraps determines the length of the knot. Needle up at **A** to begin stitching. Needle down at **B** (the location of the opposite end of the bullion) and back up at **A**, leaving a long loop of thread hanging down temporarily. Wrap this loop of thread around the needle, being careful to place the wraps side by side rather than allowing them to overlap each other. Create enough wraps to equal the space between **B** and **C** to make a straight bullion or create more wraps than this space needs to create a curved bullion stitch. Hold the wraps down with your opposite hand and pull the needle through. This will cause the thread to travel through the series of wraps as you pull tightly. Needle down at **C** (close to the **A** position) to secure the knot in place.

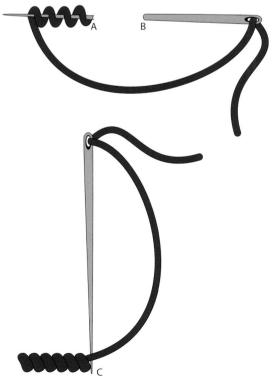

Detached Chain Stitch

Detached Chain Stitch is an individual stitch, but when grouped in a continuous line, it creates a chain effect. Needle up at **A** and down at **B** (close to the **A** position, or even the same hole); then needle up at **C**. The distance between **B** and **C** determines the length of the stitch. Needle down at **D** (crossing over the thread) to tack the loop in place. Pulling the thread loop will create a thin Chain Stitch; leaving the loop relaxed before you tack it down will create a wide Chain Stitch.

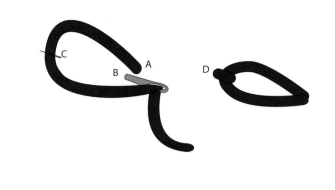

The stitching instructions for Detached Chain Stitch are the same for ribbon or thread. However, manipulate the ribbon so it continues to lie flat against the fabric: Flip it over to curve around the needle; then flip it back over to lie flat again and to create a slight point at the end for petals and leaves. Also, tack the ribbon in place with a longer tack stitch than you would use for thread if you desire the ribbon to remain lying flat.

French Knot Stitch

Needle up at **A**. Hold the thread taught with the opposite hand and wrap it around the needle. The number of wraps will determine the size of the knot; most designs in this book use 2 wraps. Needle down at **B** (which is slightly to the left of the **A** position but *not* the same hole). Pull the thread to push the wraps down against the fabric, keeping them on the needle as well. Hold the knot in place with your opposite hand and push the needle through the fabric.

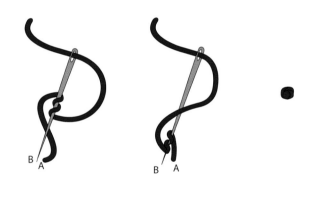

Ribbon knots can become very troublesome if they are tight since the chenille needle has such a large eye. Keep the wraps loose until you pull the ribbon through the fabric layers. The amount of pulling and the number of wraps will determine the size of the knot. The stitch motion is the same for thread or ribbon.

Loop Stitch

Needle up at **A** and down at **B** (very close to **A** but not the same hole). Leave the loop loose and do not tighten the stitch all the way through the fabric. Manipulate the ribbon as you pull it through the fabric to keep it flat rather than allowing it to twist. To create Loop Stitches that are uniform in height, slide a laying object (a straw or the like) through the loop as you pull the ribbon through. Leave the laying object in place until you are creating a subsequent stitch. It is handy to have multiple laying objects of the same type and size available to prevent the accidental *pull through* of stitches by mistake.

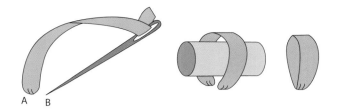

tip Secure ribbon loops by creating small tack stitches with sewing thread of a matching color to the ribbon. This prevents the loops from pulling out as the block is handled in the future.

Ribbon Stitch

This stitch is also known as the *Japanese Ribbon Stitch*. Needle up at **A**, and then pierce the ribbon as you needle down at **B**. Pull the ribbon until it curls upon itself as it goes through the hole. Stop when the curl is pleasing for your specific application. Do not let the curl completely disappear on to the back of the work by pulling the ribbon too tightly.

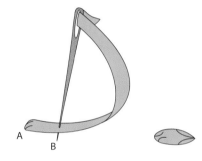

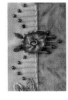

tip Ribbon Stitches can easily pull through to the back of the fabric, so use sewing thread to tack the tips of these stitches as you work. If you do pull too much and the tip curve pulls through, repeat the stitch by needling up at **A** again and place the new stitch on top of the old one. It will cover the other work nicely.

Running Stitch

Needle up at **A** to begin stitching. Then needle down at **B** and up at **C**. Skip a space equal to the length of the stitch and proceed. Repeat to create a line of stitches having equal length and spacing between them.

Stem Stitch

Begin a line of stitching with a tiny Straight Stitch (needle up at **A** and down at **C**) that is half the length of a single Stem Stitch. Needle back up at **A** to begin creating the Stem Stitches. Needle down at **B** and up at **C**, keeping the thread below the needle and stitching from right to left. If you begin and end the line of Stem Stitches with a tiny Straight Stitch (shown in red in the illustration), the line of stitching remains the same width throughout rather than tapering off at the ends.

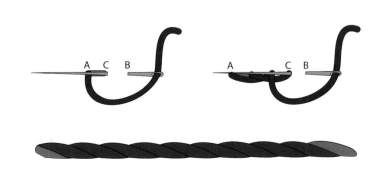

Creating Flowers

Combinations of various stitches (and beads) produce several different types of flowers. Some are good mimics of nature and others are fantasy creations. The seam diagrams (see 480 Seam Designs Organized by Base-Seam Stitch Type, page 64) include different color ideas for these flower types.

The individual stitches are diagrammed to show their position in forming the specific flower. Several flowers have centers that can be stitched as French Knots (page 38) or created with small beads.

Bullion Stitch Rose

This flower is illustrated using perle fibers for the embroidery work. The center of the flower can be a cluster of French Knots (page 38), a trio or single bead, or any other object you could surround with the Bullion Stitches (page 37). Begin the outer ring(s) of petals inside the prior petal's curve to create a spiral effect. Grouping a few stitches creates a bud or fantasy-style flower.

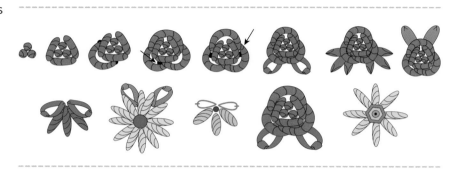

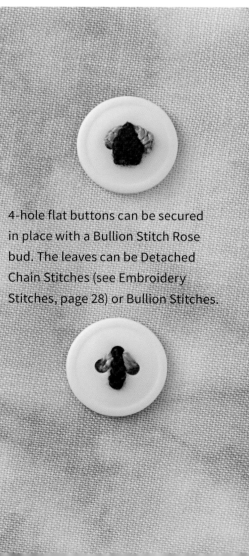

4-hole flat buttons can be secured in place with a Bullion Stitch Rose bud. The leaves can be Detached Chain Stitches (see Embroidery Stitches, page 28) or Bullion Stitches.

Daisy

Multiple Detached Chain Stitches (page 38) create a daisy-type flower when grouped into a circle or a closed daisy when grouped in a fan shape. A single stitch can represent a bud or a leaf. These can be created in thread fibers or silk ribbon.

Fargo Rose

A French Knot (page 38) and Running Stitch (page 39) are used to create this rose. The French Knot twists can be as close as 2″ from the fabric or as much as 6″ from the fabric, depending on how many petals you desire. This distance is determined by the length of ribbon to be gathered, which in turn determines the number of petals formed as the ribbon is pulled through the knots and gathers into the fabric foundation. Needle up at the base of the flower before forming the knot wraps and gathering stitches; then needle down close to the base and through the fabric.

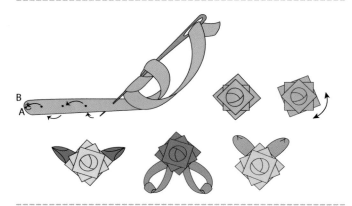

Hyacinth

French Knots (page 38) can be arranged to create a realistic flower mimicking a hyacinth, lilac, baby's breath, or other blossom having multiple tiny buds. Clusters can also create the center of larger flower blossoms. When stitching this cluster of French Knots, begin with the long centerline of knots; then add the knots on the side. Lastly, add the extra knots at the top. This stitching sequence will help to create multiple uniformly sized flowers.

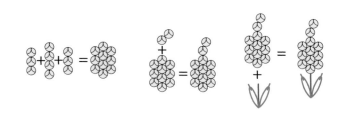

Iris

The iris flower is a combination of stitches. This is a tall flower, with the top portion of the flower head being about one-third the total height and the arms of the flower head being the second third of the total height. The leaves should be tall and cover one-half the total height. Begin by stitching a full, slightly puffy Detached Chain Stitch (page 38) for the head. If the stitch is very open in the center, add a Straight Stitch (page 34) underneath to fill in the space. The arms of the flower are formed with a *single* Straight Stitch in the shape of an upside-down horseshoe. They should begin far enough below the base of flower top to, in effect, double the size of the flower's top portion. Start on one side; travel the ribbon up, lying flat; and slide the eye of the needle under the iris head while manipulating the ribbon to turn and then lie flat against the surface. Curve the ribbon, turning it downward, and needle down at a point opposite the first needle up of the stitch. Add leaves in either a Ribbon Stitch or Straight Stitch, and add a stem embroidered with thread.

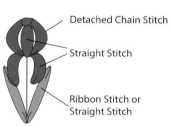

Detached Chain Stitch

Straight Stitch

Ribbon Stitch or Straight Stitch

Ribbon Stitch Flower

Pairs or trios of Ribbon Stitches (page 39) make simple leaf clusters for small flower heads like the Woven Rose, Stem Stitch Rose, and Straight-Stitch Flowers. The ribbon can be pierced at the center or slightly to one side when creating a Ribbon Stitch. Combinations of long Ribbon Stitches with side pierced needle positions create interesting fan shapes.

Stem Stitch Rose

The center of the flower can be a knot, a large bead, or any other object than can be surrounded with petals. The center commonly sits at the top of the flower, and the petals are created in rows of Stem Stitches (page 39) that travel from left to right, partially around the center. Each row is longer than the previous since it also travels around the prior row of petals. The last row can be shortened so that it only sits under the center portion of the previous row, especially for larger flowers in this variety. Stitching completely around the center in a circle can create another variety of this flower.

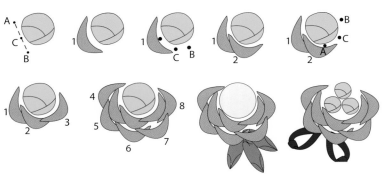

Straight–Stitch Flower

Each Straight Stitch (page 34) represents a single petal on the flower. Place the individual Straight Stitches so that they overlap as needed to mimic the chosen flower shape. You can easily create variations by substituting Ribbon Stitches (page 39) or Detached Chain Stitches (page 38) for these Straight Stitches. Groups of stitches can be combined to also form fan shapes, butterflies, or circles.

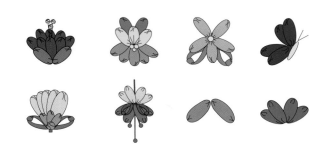

Woven Rose

Weave ribbon or thread over and under with an odd number of Straight Stitches (page 34), all of which will meet in the center to create a Woven Rose. When using ribbon, variations can be easily achieved by pulling the ribbon tight or keeping the weaving loose, or by keeping the ribbon flat or letting it twist. The size of an individual Woven Rose is determined by the length of the spokes (Straight Stitches) created as its base for weaving. Use a tapestry (blunt-end) needle for weaving or the eye end of the chenille needle.

Wrapped Rose

Create petals by wrapping Straight Stitches (page 34) in ribbon to produce more bulk. Complete each single petal before continuing to the next petal. Use the eye end of the chenille needle after creating the Straight Stitch to wrap the ribbon by sliding the eye under the stitch. Continue to wrap until the bulk desired is reached; then needle down at **B** to complete the wraps. A tapestry needle can be used for the wrapping, but you'll need to unthread and rethread the needle to change from the chenille to the tapestry needle. The length of the Straight Stitch and the number of wraps will determine the size of the finished rose.

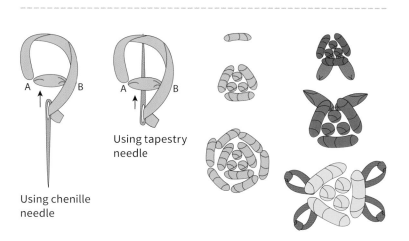

Using chenille needle

Using tapestry needle

Creating Shapes and Objects

Shapes can be created by clustering stitches together just as flowers are. Circles, half-circles, fans, and other objects require only simple stitches in thread fibers and/or silk ribbon to mimic recognizable things.

Bees and Flies

Bumblebees are created using gold, yellow, and black thread. The bodies can be created with beads or Bullion Stitches (page 37). Alternate the knots in gold and black colors to create a striped effect on the body. The wings can be simple Detached Chain Stitches (page 38) in thread or Straight Stitches (page 34) if done in ribbon. Change your colors to browns or greens for flies and other types of bees.

Butterflies

Pairing some Straight Stitches (page 34) in silk ribbon or Detached Chain Stitches (page 38) in thread or ribbon creates tiny butterflies. A rice-shaped bead or Bullion Stitch (page 37) is used as the body.

Circles and Fans

Fan, circle, and half-circle shapes add interest to seams, especially when several weights and colors of thread are used. Straight Stitches (page 34), Back Stitches (page 37), and Detached Chain Stitches (page 38) combine to define the main parts. *Note:* The Detached Chain Stitches used here have a wider base; **A** and **B** are set farther apart than usual. Finally, add silk ribbon flowers and beads to dress the shape up.

Hearts

Add hearts to seams or use them as small motifs. Various heart sizes can be drawn on fabric and then covered with Straight Stitches (page 34). A heart template design is included in the base-seam templates (see Templates for Base Seams, page 22). Adding flowers or beads to the stitched heart design can turn a simple idea into a romantic motif.

Loop Pendants

Loop Stitches (page 39) are combined with beads to create a pendant shape. The number, size, and color of beads can be varied, as can the size of ribbon used for the loops.

Prongs

Clusters of Straight Stitches (page 34) create prongs for many of these seam designs. These clusters may be an odd or even number of stitches. The specific location of the needle-up and needle-down positions for each Straight Stitch are indicated by the beginning and end of each drawn line. The angle of these Straight Stitches is easy to identify if you consider some imaginary lines as you view them.

The most common of these prong groups is the 5-prong group, and there are 2 template design sizes for this cluster (see Templates for Base Seams, page 22). Omit some of these prongs to adapt this guide to a 3-prong group easily.

When stitching this cluster, begin with the longest center prong. Needle up at the outer point and then down at the base. This center prong of the 5-prong cluster should be a vertical stitch at a 90° angle from the base seamline.

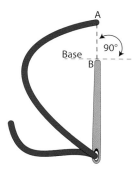

All other prongs will also be stitched from their outer point into the base, thereby continually piercing the prior work as you repeatedly needle down into this center base position. This piercing will lock the previous stitches in place and also keep them from pulling back to the front since the stitch motion is always down through the fabric layers.

The 2 outermost prongs are oriented at a 45° angle between the center prong and the base seamline.

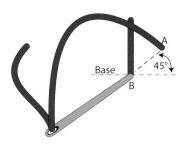

The last 2 prongs to be stitched in this 5-prong group begin at a point visually aligned between the center and outermost prong on each side. Visualize an imaginary line between these 2 prongs and place the newly stitched prong beginning at the center of this imaginary line; end the stitch at the center base.

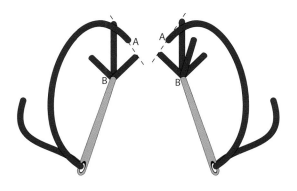

Web prongs include a trio of Straight Stitches (page 34) across the base of 5 prongs. Cross over the center long stitch in the prong base and keep the trio of stitches on each side close together.

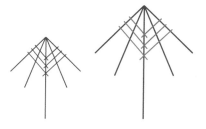

Other Straight-Stitch prongs will generally follow a repetitive pattern like the 5-prong cluster. Stitch each from the outside tip to the base for each of the Straight Stitches. Consider each cluster group to identify the angle of each individual Straight Stitch (90°, 45°, and so on) to freehand stitch each group uniformly. Template designs for fans, circles, hearts, and common prong groups are included (see Templates for Base Seams, page 22).

Pumpkins

Round items like pumpkins (or apples and the like) are created with large Bullion Stitches (page 37). You can create variations on this idea by couching down cording or substituting Wrapped Straight Stitches (page 34).

Spiders

These are a traditional motif to use in crazy quilts. Adding tiny spiders to a seam is one way to incorporate them into a project. They are especially interesting when combined with the 5-prong web cluster of Straight Stitches (page 49). Beads or varied sizes of French Knots (page 38) make the spider's body, while simple single-ply thread Straight Stitches (page 34) create the legs.

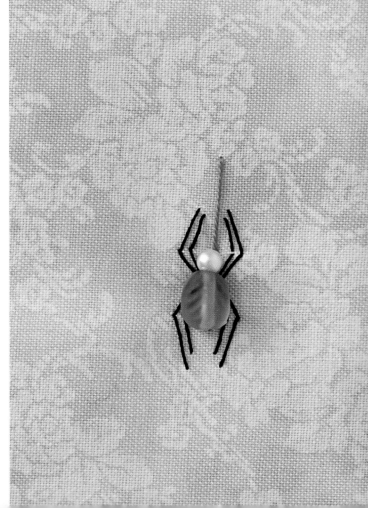

Gallery of Seam Designs

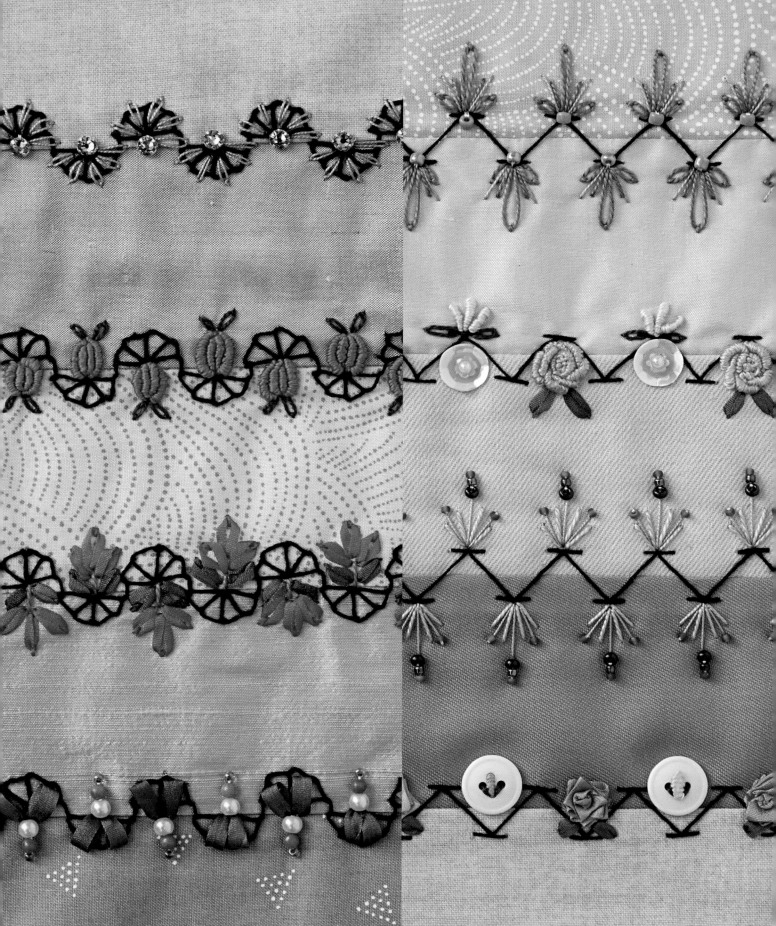

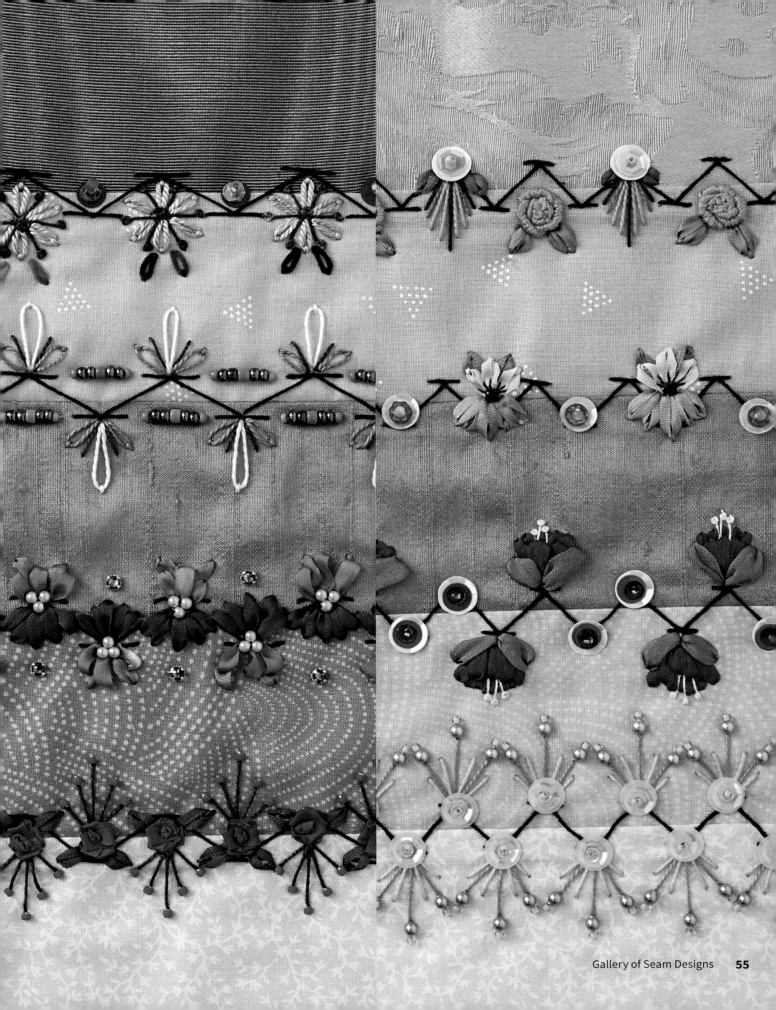

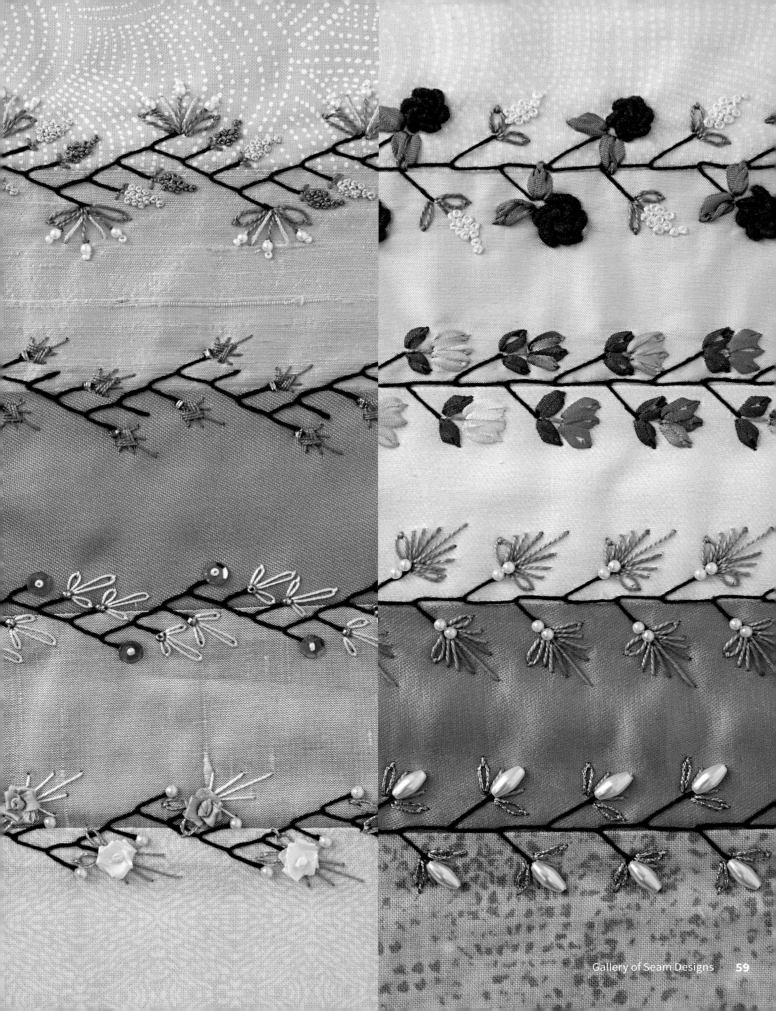

480 Seam Designs
Organized by Base-Seam Stitch Type

Full-color seam-design diagrams are organized based on the type of base-seam embroidery stitch used. These illustrations also contain a brief narrative of supplies to consider when creating the design of each individual seam. Your personal taste and available stash of supplies may cause the substitution or elimination of some of the elements within each design when you create your own version.

The size of a stitched seam will be different from the size of the diagrams shown, as each has been enlarged to clearly show the various stitches, flowers, beads, and baubles considered in the individual design.

Blanket Stitch Base-Seam Designs

1 **Base-seam template:** Blanket Stitch Base Seam 1; **Thread embroidery stitches:** Blanket Stitch, Bullion Stitch; **Silk ribbon embroidery stitches:** Ribbon Stitch; **Beads and baubles:** 3 mm round bead

2 **Base-seam template:** Blanket Stitch Base Seam 1; **Thread embroidery stitches:** Blanket Stitch, Straight Stitch; **Silk ribbon embroidery stitches:** Straight Stitch, Detached Chain Stitch, French Knot; **Beads and baubles:** 3 mm rice bead

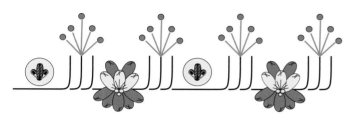

3 **Base-seam template:** Blanket Stitch Base Seam 1; **Thread embroidery stitches:** Blanket Stitch, Straight Stitch, Detached Chain Stitch, Bullion Stitch; **Silk ribbon embroidery stitches:** Straight Stitch; **Beads and baubles:** 3 mm round bead, size 15 rocailles, button

4 **Base-seam template:** Blanket Stitch Base Seam 1; **Thread embroidery stitches:** Blanket Stitch, Straight Stitch; **Silk ribbon embroidery stitches:** Ribbon Stitch, French Knot, Stem Stitch Rose, Straight Stitch, Detached Chain Stitch; **Beads and baubles:** 3 mm round bead, seed bead

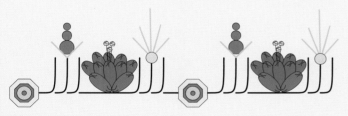

5 **Base-seam template:** Blanket Stitch Base Seam 1; **Thread embroidery stitches:** Blanket Stitch, Straight Stitch, French Knot; **Silk ribbon embroidery stitches:** Straight Stitch; **Beads and baubles:** 3 mm round bead, 2 mm round bead, seed bead, sequin

6 **Base-seam template:** Blanket Stitch Base Seam 1; **Thread embroidery stitches:** Blanket Stitch, Straight Stitch; **Silk ribbon embroidery stitches:** Ribbon Stitch, Detached Chain Stitch, French Knot; **Beads and baubles:** 4-hole button, 3 mm round bead

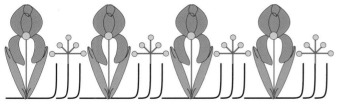

7 **Base-seam template:** Blanket Stitch Base Seam 1; **Thread embroidery stitches:** Blanket Stitch, Straight Stitch, French Knot; **Silk ribbon embroidery stitches:** Detached Chain Stitch, Straight Stitch, Ribbon Stitch; **Beads and baubles:** Seed bead

8 **Base-seam template:** Blanket Stitch Base Seam 1; **Thread embroidery stitches:** Blanket Stitch, Bullion Stitch; **Silk ribbon embroidery stitches:** Detached Chain; **Beads and baubles:** 3 mm and 4 mm round beads

9 **Base-seam template:** Blanket Stitch Base Seam 1; **Thread embroidery stitches:** Blanket Stitch; **Silk ribbon embroidery stitches:** Ribbon Stitch, Straight Stitch, Detached Chain Stitch; **Beads and baubles:** Seed bead, sequin

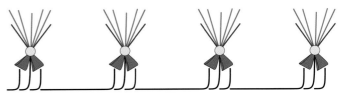

10 **Base-seam template:** Blanket Stitch Base Seam 2; **Thread embroidery stitches:** Blanket Stitch, Straight Stitch; **Silk ribbon embroidery stitches:** Loop Stitch; **Beads and baubles:** 3 mm round bead

11 **Base-seam template:** Blanket Stitch Base Seam 2; **Thread embroidery stitches:** Blanket Stitch, Detached Chain Stitch, French Knot, Straight Stitch; **Silk ribbon embroidery stitches:** Straight Stitch; **Beads and baubles:** Seed bead, rice bead

12 **Base-seam template:** Blanket Stitch Base Seam 2; **Thread embroidery stitches:** Blanket Stitch, Straight Stitch; **Silk ribbon embroidery stitches:** Woven Rose, Ribbon Stitch, Straight Stitch; **Beads and baubles:** 3 mm crystal montée, rice bead

13 **Base-seam template:** Blanket Stitch Base Seam 2; **Thread embroidery stitches:** Blanket Stitch; **Silk ribbon embroidery stitches:** Stem Stitch Rose, Ribbon Stitch, French Knot, Detached Chain Stitch; **Beads and baubles:** 3 mm round bead, seed bead

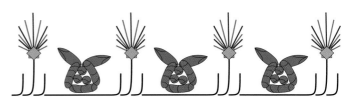

14 **Base-seam template:** Blanket Stitch Base Seam 2; **Thread embroidery stitches:** Blanket Stitch, Straight Stitch; **Silk ribbon embroidery stitches:** Wrapped Straight Stitch Rose, French Knot, Ribbon Stitch; **Beads and baubles:** 3 mm crystal montée

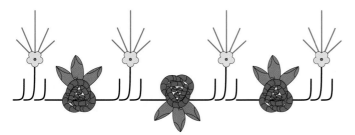

15 **Base-seam template:** Blanket Stitch Base Seam 2; **Thread embroidery stitches:** Blanket Stitch, Straight Stitch, Bullion Knot Stitch, French Knot; **Silk ribbon embroidery stitches:** Ribbon Stitch; **Beads and baubles:** 5 mm flower cap bead, seed bead

16 **Base-seam template:** Blanket Stitch Base Seam 2; **Thread embroidery stitches:** Blanket Stitch, Straight Stitch; **Silk ribbon embroidery stitches:** Ribbon Stitch, Detached Chain Stitch, French Knot; **Beads and baubles:** 3 mm crystal montée

17 Base-seam template: Blanket Stitch Base Seam 2;
Thread embroidery stitches: Blanket Stitch, Straight Stitch;
Silk ribbon embroidery stitches: Straight Stitch, Ribbon Stitch, Detached Chain Stitch; **Beads and baubles:** Button

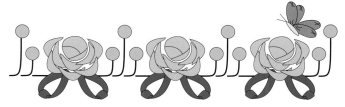

18 Base-seam template: Blanket Stitch Base Seam 2;
Thread embroidery stitches: Blanket Stitch, Straight Stitch; **Silk ribbon embroidery stitches:** Straight Stitch, French Knot, Detached Chain Stitch, Stem Stitch Rose; **Beads and baubles:** 4 mm round bead, 3 mm rice bead

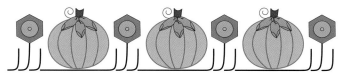

19 Base-seam template: Blanket Stitch Base Seam 2;
Thread embroidery stitches: Blanket Stitch, Bullion Stitch, Back Stitch; **Silk ribbon embroidery stitches:** Ribbon Stitch; **Beads and baubles:** Seed bead, sequin

20 Base-seam template: Blanket Stitch Base Seam 2;
Thread embroidery stitches: Blanket Stitch, Straight Stitch, Detached Chain Stitch; **Silk ribbon embroidery stitches:** None; **Beads and baubles:** 3 mm round bead

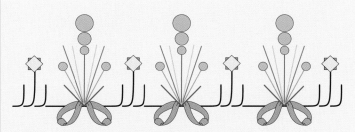

21 Base-seam template: Blanket Stitch Base Seam 2;
Thread embroidery stitches: Blanket Stitch, Straight Stitch;
Silk ribbon embroidery stitches: Detached Chain Stitch;
Beads and baubles: 4 mm crystal montée, 4 mm round bead, 3 mm round bead, seed bead

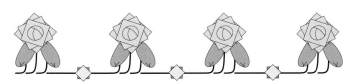

22 Base-seam template: Blanket Stitch Base Seam 2;
Thread embroidery stitches: Blanket Stitch; **Silk ribbon embroidery stitches:** Straight Stitch, Fargo Rose; **Beads and baubles:** 3 mm montée

23 Base-seam template: Blanket Stitch Base Seam 2;
Thread embroidery stitches: Blanket Stitch, Straight Stitch;
Silk ribbon embroidery stitches: Straight Stitch, Detached Chain Stitch; **Beads and baubles:** 3 mm round bead

24 Base-seam template: Blanket Stitch Base Seam 2;
Thread embroidery stitches: Blanket Stitch; **Silk ribbon embroidery stitches:** Straight Stitch, Detached Chain Stitch; **Beads and baubles:** Seed bead, 3 mm round bead

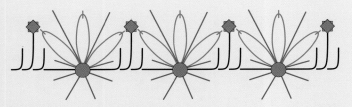

25 **Base-seam template:** Blanket Stitch Base Seam 2;
Thread embroidery stitches: Blanket Stitch, Straight Stitch,
Detached Chain Stitch; **Silk ribbon embroidery stitches:** None;
Beads and baubles: 3 mm crystal montée, 4 mm round bead

26 **Base-seam template:** Blanket Stitch Base Seam 2;
Thread embroidery stitches: Blanket Stitch; **Silk ribbon
embroidery stitches:** Fargo Rose, Detached Chain Stitch;
Beads and baubles: 4 mm flower cap bead, seed bead

27 **Base-seam template:** Blanket Stitch Base Seam 2;
Thread embroidery stitches: Blanket Stitch, Straight Stitch;
Silk ribbon embroidery stitches: Detached Chain Stitch;
Beads and baubles: Button

28 **Base-seam template:** Blanket Stitch Base Seam 2; **Thread
embroidery stitches:** Blanket Stitch, Straight Stitch, French
Knot; **Silk ribbon embroidery stitches:** Ribbon Stitch, Straight
Stitch, Detached Chain Stitch; **Beads and baubles:** None

29 **Base-seam template:** Blanket Stitch Base Seam 2;
Thread embroidery stitches: Blanket Stitch, Bullion Stitch,
French Knot, Detached Chain Stitch; **Silk ribbon embroidery
stitches:** Straight Stitch, Detached Chain Stitch; **Beads and
baubles:** 3 mm rice bead

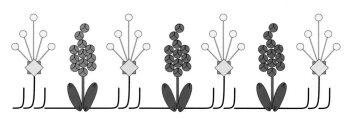

30 **Base-seam template:** Blanket Stitch Base Seam 2;
Thread embroidery stitches: Blanket Stitch, French Knot,
Straight Stitch; **Silk ribbon embroidery stitches:** Straight
Stitch; **Beads and baubles:** Seed bead, 4 mm montée

31 **Base-seam template:** Blanket Stitch Base Seam 2;
Thread embroidery stitches: Blanket Stitch; **Silk ribbon
embroidery stitches:** Straight Stitch, Woven Rose; **Beads
and baubles:** 4 mm rice bead

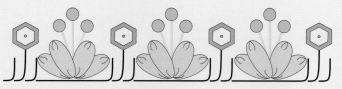

32 **Base-seam template:** Blanket Stitch Base Seam 2;
Thread embroidery stitches: Blanket Stitch, Straight Stitch;
Silk ribbon embroidery stitches: Straight Stitch; **Beads and
baubles:** Seed bead, sequin, 3 mm round bead

33 **Base-seam template:** Blanket Stitch Base Seam 2;
Thread embroidery stitches: Blanket Stitch, Bullion Stitch;
Silk ribbon embroidery stitches: Detached Chain Stitch;
Beads and baubles: Seed bead, sequin, 4 mm round bead

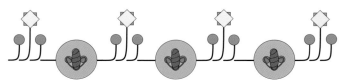

34 **Base-seam template:** Blanket Stitch Base Seam 2; **Thread
embroidery stitches:** Blanket Stitch, Detached Chain Stitch,
Bullion Stitch; **Silk ribbon embroidery stitches:** None; **Beads
and baubles:** 3 mm round bead, 4 mm montée, 4-hole button

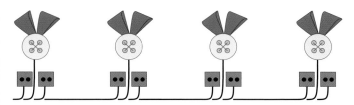

35 **Base-seam template:** Blanket Stitch Base Seam 2;
Thread embroidery stitches: Blanket Stitch; **Silk ribbon
embroidery stitches:** Loop Stitch; **Beads and baubles:**
Square and round button

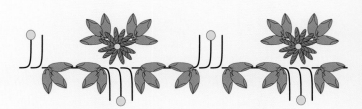

36 **Base-seam template:** Blanket Stitch Base Seam 3;
Thread embroidery stitches: Blanket Stitch, Bullion Stitch;
Silk ribbon embroidery stitches: Ribbon Stitch; **Beads and
baubles:** 3 mm round bead, seed bead

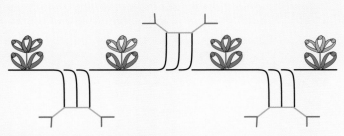

37 **Base-seam template:** Blanket Stitch Base Seam 3;
Thread embroidery stitches: Blanket Stitch, Straight Stitch;
Silk ribbon embroidery stitches: Detached Chain Stitch;
Beads and baubles: None

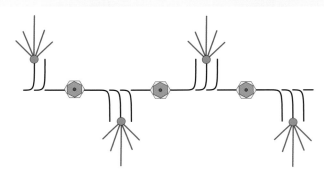

38 **Base-seam template:** Blanket Stitch Base Seam 3; **Thread
embroidery stitches:** Blanket Stitch, Straight Stitch; **Silk ribbon
embroidery stitches:** None; **Beads and baubles:** Seed bead,
sequin, 3 mm round bead

39 **Base-seam template:** Blanket Stitch Base Seam 3; **Thread
embroidery stitches:** Blanket Stitch, Straight Stitch; **Silk ribbon
embroidery stitches:** Straight Stitch; **Beads and baubles:** Seed
bead, 2 mm round bead, 3 mm round bead, size 15 rocailles

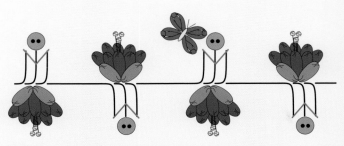

40 **Base-seam template:** Blanket Stitch Base Seam 3;
Thread embroidery stitches: Blanket Stitch, Straight Stitch,
French Knot; **Silk ribbon embroidery stitches:** Straight Stitch,
Detached Chain Stitch; **Beads and baubles:** Rice bead, button

41 **Base-seam template:** Blanket Stitch Base Seam 3; **Thread embroidery stitches:** Blanket Stitch, Straight Stitch; **Silk ribbon embroidery stitches:** Detached Chain Stitch; **Beads and baubles:** 4 mm round bead

42 **Base-seam template:** Blanket Stitch Base Seam 3; **Thread embroidery stitches:** Blanket Stitch; **Silk ribbon embroidery stitches:** Detached Chain Stitch, Fargo Rose; **Beads and baubles:** None

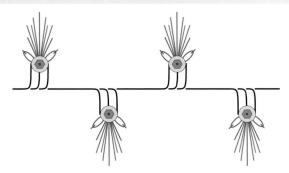

43 **Base-seam template:** Blanket Stitch Base Seam 3; **Thread embroidery stitches:** Blanket Stitch, Straight Stitch, Detached Chain Stitch; **Silk ribbon embroidery stitches:** None; **Beads and baubles:** Seed bead, sequin

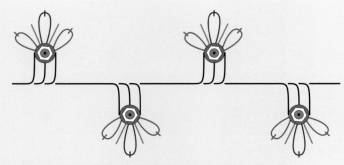

44 **Base-seam template:** Blanket Stitch Base Seam 3; **Thread embroidery stitches:** Blanket Stitch, Straight Stitch, Detached Chain Stitch; **Silk ribbon embroidery stitches:** None; **Beads and baubles:** Seed bead, sequin

45 **Base-seam template:** Blanket Stitch Base Seam 3; **Thread embroidery stitches:** Blanket Stitch, Straight Stitch, Detached Chain Stitch; **Silk ribbon embroidery stitches:** Detached Chain Stitch, Fargo Rose; **Beads and baubles:** 2 mm round bead

46 **Base-seam template:** Blanket Stitch Base Seam 3; **Thread embroidery stitches:** Blanket Stitch, Straight Stitch; **Silk ribbon embroidery stitches:** Detached Chain Stitch, Straight Stitch; **Beads and baubles:** Rice bead, 3 mm round bead

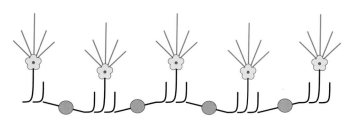

47 **Base-seam template:** Blanket Stitch Base Seam 4; **Thread embroidery stitches:** Blanket Stitch, Straight Stitch; **Silk ribbon embroidery stitches:** None; **Beads and baubles:** Flower cap bead, seed bead, 3 mm round bead

48 **Base-seam template:** Blanket Stitch Base Seam 4; **Thread embroidery stitches:** Blanket Stitch, Straight Stitch, Detached Chain Stitch; **Silk ribbon embroidery stitches:** Straight Stitch, French Knot, Detached Chain Stitch; **Beads and baubles:** Seed bead

49 **Base-seam template:** Blanket Stitch Base Seam 4;
Thread embroidery stitches: Blanket Stitch, Straight Stitch,
Detached Chain Stitch; **Silk ribbon embroidery stitches:**
None; **Beads and baubles:** 2 mm round bead

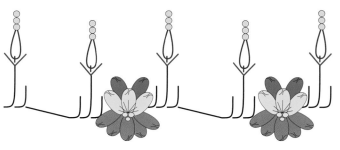

50 **Base-seam template:** Blanket Stitch Base Seam 4;
Thread embroidery stitches: Blanket Stitch, Straight Stitch,
Detached Chain Stitch; **Silk ribbon embroidery stitches:**
Straight Stitch; **Beads and baubles:** Seed bead, size 15 rocailles

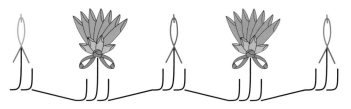

51 **Base-seam template:** Blanket Stitch Base Seam 4; **Thread
embroidery stitches:** Blanket Stitch, Straight Stitch, Detached
Chain Stitch; **Silk ribbon embroidery stitches:** Ribbon Stitch,
Detached Chain Stitch, French Knot; **Beads and baubles:** None

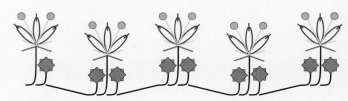

52 **Base-seam template:** Blanket Stitch Base Seam 4;
Thread embroidery stitches: Blanket Stitch, Straight Stitch,
Detached Chain Stitch; **Silk ribbon embroidery stitches:**
None; **Beads and baubles:** 4 mm montée, 2 mm round bead

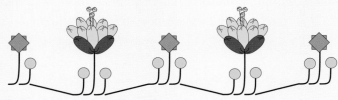

53 **Base-seam template:** Blanket Stitch Base Seam 4;
Thread embroidery stitches: Blanket Stitch, Straight Stitch,
French Knot; **Silk ribbon embroidery stitches:** Straight
Stitch; **Beads and baubles:** 4 mm montée, 3 mm round bead

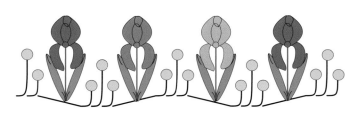

54 **Base-seam template:** Blanket Stitch Base Seam 4;
Thread embroidery stitches: Blanket Stitch, Straight Stitch;
Silk ribbon embroidery stitches: Straight Stitch, Ribbon Stitch,
Detached Chain Stitch; **Beads and baubles:** 3 mm round bead

55 **Base-seam template:** Blanket Stitch Base Seam 4;
Thread embroidery stitches: Blanket Stitch, Straight
Stitch; **Silk ribbon embroidery stitches:** Straight Stitch;
Beads and baubles: 2 mm round bead, size 15 rocailles

56 **Base-seam template:** Blanket Stitch Base Seam 4; **Thread
embroidery stitches:** Blanket Stitch; **Silk ribbon embroidery
stitches:** Straight Stitch, Ribbon Stitch, Detached Chain Stitch;
Beads and baubles: 3 mm round bead

57 **Base-seam template:** Blanket Stitch Base Seam 4; **Thread embroidery stitches:** Blanket Stitch; **Silk ribbon embroidery stitches:** Loop Stitch; **Beads and baubles:** Rice bead, 3 mm round bead

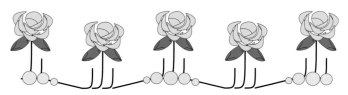

58 **Base-seam template:** Blanket Stitch Base Seam 4; **Thread embroidery stitches:** Blanket Stitch; **Silk ribbon embroidery stitches:** Ribbon Stitch, Stem Stitch Rose, French Knot; **Beads and baubles:** Seed bead, 2 mm round bead, 3 mm round bead

59 **Base-seam template:** Blanket Stitch Base Seam 4; **Thread embroidery stitches:** Blanket Stitch; **Silk ribbon embroidery stitches:** Detached Chain Stitch, Woven Rose; **Beads and baubles:** 3 mm round bead

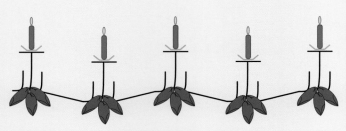

60 **Base-seam template:** Blanket Stitch Base Seam 4; **Thread embroidery stitches:** Blanket Stitch, Straight Stitch; **Silk ribbon embroidery stitches:** Ribbon Stitch; **Beads and baubles:** Rice bead, bugle bead

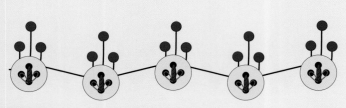

61 **Base-seam template:** Blanket Stitch Base Seam 4; **Thread embroidery stitches:** Blanket Stitch, Detached Chain Stitch, Bullion Stitch; **Silk ribbon embroidery stitches:** None; **Beads and baubles:** 4-hole button, 3 mm round bead

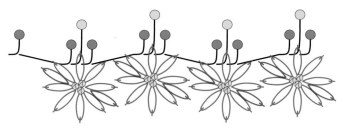

62 **Base-seam template:** Blanket Stitch Base Seam 4; **Thread embroidery stitches:** Blanket Stitch, Detached Chain Stitch, French Knot; **Silk ribbon embroidery stitches:** None; **Beads and baubles:** 3 mm round bead

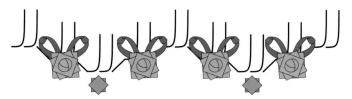

63 **Base-seam template:** Blanket Stitch Base Seam 5; **Thread embroidery stitches:** Blanket Stitch; **Silk ribbon embroidery stitches:** Detached Chain Stitch, Fargo Rose; **Beads and baubles:** 3 mm montée

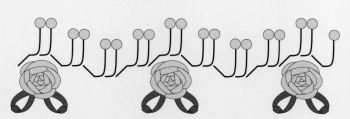

64 **Base-seam template:** Blanket Stitch Base Seam 5; **Thread embroidery stitches:** Blanket Stitch; **Silk ribbon embroidery stitches:** Detached Chain Stitch, Woven Rose; **Beads and baubles:** 3 mm round bead

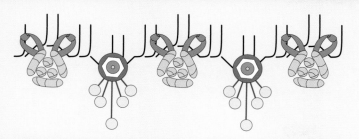

65 **Base-seam template:** Blanket Stitch Base Seam 5; **Thread embroidery stitches:** Blanket Stitch, Straight Stitch; **Silk ribbon embroidery stitches:** Wrapped Straight Stitch, French Knot, Detached Chain Stitch; **Beads and baubles:** Seed bead, sequin, 3 mm round bead

66 **Base-seam template:** Blanket Stitch Base Seam 5; **Thread embroidery stitches:** Blanket Stitch, Straight Stitch; **Silk ribbon embroidery stitches:** Straight Stitch, Detached Chain Stitch; **Beads and baubles:** Seed bead

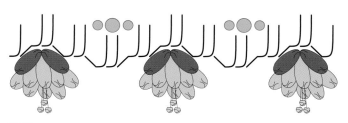

67 **Base-seam template:** Blanket Stitch Base Seam 5; **Thread embroidery stitches:** Blanket Stitch, French Knot, Straight Stitch; **Silk ribbon embroidery stitches:** Straight Stitch; **Beads and baubles:** 2 mm round bead, 4 mm round bead

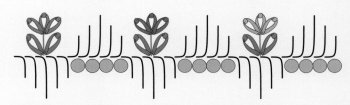

68 **Base-seam template:** Blanket Stitch Base Seam 6; **Thread embroidery stitches:** Blanket Stitch, Straight Stitch; **Silk ribbon embroidery stitches:** Detached Chain Stitch; **Beads and baubles:** 4 mm round bead

69 **Base-seam template:** Blanket Stitch Base Seam 6; **Thread embroidery stitches:** Blanket Stitch, Straight Stitch; **Silk ribbon embroidery stitches:** Straight Stitch; **Beads and baubles:** Rice bead, button

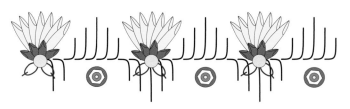

70 **Base-seam template:** Blanket Stitch Base Seam 6; **Thread embroidery stitches:** Blanket Stitch, Detached Chain Stitch; **Silk ribbon embroidery stitches:** Ribbon Stitch; **Beads and baubles:** Seed bead, sequin, 4 mm round bead

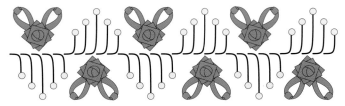

71 **Base-seam template:** Blanket Stitch Base Seam 6; **Thread embroidery stitches:** Blanket Stitch; **Silk ribbon embroidery stitches:** Fargo Rose, Detached Chain Stitch; **Beads and baubles:** Seed bead

72 **Base-seam template:** Blanket Stitch Base Seam 6; **Thread embroidery stitches:** Blanket Stitch; **Silk ribbon embroidery stitches:** Straight Stitch, Ribbon Stitch, Detached Chain Stitch; **Beads and baubles:** Bugle bead

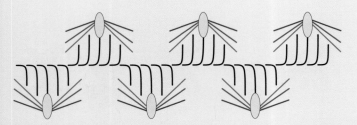

73 **Base-seam template:** Blanket Stitch Base Seam 6; **Thread embroidery stitches:** Blanket Stitch, Straight Stitch; **Silk ribbon embroidery stitches:** None; **Beads and baubles:** Rice bead

74 **Base-seam template:** Blanket Stitch Base Seam 7; **Thread embroidery stitches:** Blanket Stitch; **Silk ribbon embroidery stitches:** Straight Stitch, Ribbon Stitch, Detached Chain Stitch; **Beads and baubles:** None

75 **Base-seam template:** Blanket Stitch Base Seam 7; **Thread embroidery stitches:** Blanket Stitch, Straight Stitch; **Silk ribbon embroidery stitches:** Straight Stitch, Fargo Rose; **Beads and baubles:** None

76 **Base-seam template:** Blanket Stitch Base Seam 7; **Thread embroidery stitches:** Blanket Stitch; **Silk ribbon embroidery stitches:** Ribbon Stitch; **Beads and baubles:** 2 mm round bead, 4 mm round bead

77 **Base-seam template:** Blanket Stitch Base Seam 7; **Thread embroidery stitches:** Blanket Stitch, Straight Stitch; **Silk ribbon embroidery stitches:** Detached Chain Stitch; **Beads and baubles:** None

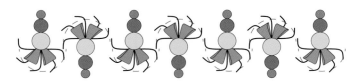

78 **Base-seam template:** Blanket Stitch Base Seam 7; **Thread embroidery stitches:** Blanket Stitch; **Silk ribbon embroidery stitches:** Loop Stitch; **Beads and baubles:** 2 mm round bead, 3 mm round bead, 4 mm round bead

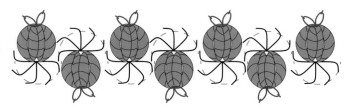

79 **Base-seam template:** Blanket Stitch Base Seam 7; **Thread embroidery stitches:** Blanket Stitch, Bullion Stitch, Detached Chain Stitch; **Silk ribbon embroidery stitches:** None; **Beads and baubles:** None

80 **Base-seam template:** Blanket Stitch Base Seam 7; **Thread embroidery stitches:** Blanket Stitch, Detached Chain Stitch; **Silk ribbon embroidery stitches:** None; **Beads and baubles:** 4 mm montée

81 **Base-seam template:** Blanket Stitch Base Seam 7; **Thread embroidery stitches:** Blanket Stitch, French Knot, Detached Chain Stitch, Straight Stitch; **Silk ribbon embroidery stitches:** None; **Beads and baubles:** None

82 **Base-seam template:** Blanket Stitch Base Seam 7; **Thread embroidery stitches:** Blanket Stitch; **Silk ribbon embroidery stitches:** Fargo Rose, Detached Chain Stitch; **Beads and baubles:** None

83 **Base-seam template:** Blanket Stitch Base Seam 7; **Thread embroidery stitches:** Blanket Stitch, Straight Stitch; **Silk ribbon embroidery stitches:** None; **Beads and baubles:** 2 mm round bead

84 **Base-seam template:** Blanket Stitch Base Seam 7; **Thread embroidery stitches:** Blanket Stitch; **Silk ribbon embroidery stitches:** None; **Beads and baubles:** Seed bead, sequin

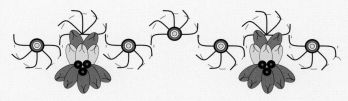

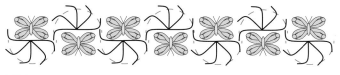

85 **Base-seam template:** Blanket Stitch Base Seam 7; **Thread embroidery stitches:** Blanket Stitch; **Silk ribbon embroidery stitches:** Ribbon Stitch; **Beads and baubles:** Seed bead, sequin

86 **Base-seam template:** Blanket Stitch Base Seam 7; **Thread embroidery stitches:** Blanket Stitch, Straight Stitch; **Silk ribbon embroidery stitches:** Straight Stitch, Detached Chain Stitch; **Beads and baubles:** Rice bead

Chevron Stitch Base-Seam Designs

87 Base-seam template: Chevron Stitch Base Seam 1;
Thread embroidery stitches: Chevron Stitch, Straight Stitch;
Silk ribbon embroidery stitches: None; **Beads and baubles:**
3 mm round bead

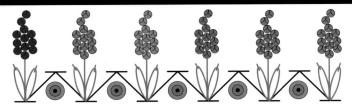

88 Base-seam template: Chevron Stitch Base Seam 1;
Thread embroidery stitches: Chevron Stitch, Straight Stitch,
Detached Chain Stitch, French Knot; **Silk ribbon embroidery
stitches:** None; **Beads and baubles:** Seed bead, sequin

89 Base-seam template: Chevron Stitch Base Seam 1; **Thread
embroidery stitches:** Chevron Stitch, Straight Stitch, Detached
Chain Stitch; **Silk ribbon embroidery stitches:** None; **Beads
and baubles:** 2 mm round bead

90 Base-seam template: Chevron Stitch Base Seam 1;
Thread embroidery stitches: Chevron Stitch, Detached
Chain Stitch; **Silk ribbon embroidery stitches:** Detached
Chain Stitch, Bullion Stitch; **Beads and baubles:** Seed
bead, sequin, 2 mm round bead

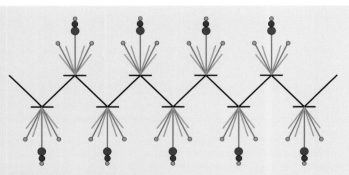

91 Base-seam template: Chevron Stitch Base Seam 1;
Thread embroidery stitches: Chevron Stitch, Straight Stitch;
Silk ribbon embroidery stitches: None; **Beads and baubles:**
Seed bead, 2 mm round bead, 3 mm round bead

92 Base-seam template: Chevron Stitch Base Seam 1;
Thread embroidery stitches: Chevron Stitch, Bullion Stitch,
Detached Chain Stitch; **Silk ribbon embroidery stitches:**
Straight Stitch, Fargo Rose; **Beads and baubles:** 4-hole button

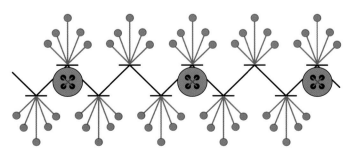

93 Base-seam template: Chevron Stitch Base Seam 1;
Thread embroidery stitches: Chevron Stitch, Straight Stitch;
Silk ribbon embroidery stitches: None; **Beads and baubles:**
Seed bead, button

94 Base-seam template: Chevron Stitch Base Seam 1;
Thread embroidery stitches: Chevron Stitch, Straight Stitch;
Silk ribbon embroidery stitches: Straight Stitch, Detached
Chain Stitch; **Beads and baubles:** Seed bead, sequin

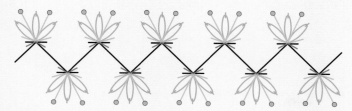

95 **Base-seam template:** Chevron Stitch Base Seam 1; **Thread embroidery stitches:** Chevron Stitch, Straight Stitch, Detached Chain Stitch; **Silk ribbon embroidery stitches:** None; **Beads and baubles:** Seed bead

96 **Base-seam template:** Chevron Stitch Base Seam 1; **Thread embroidery stitches:** Chevron Stitch; **Silk ribbon embroidery stitches:** Ribbon Stitch, Fargo Rose; **Beads and baubles:** Button

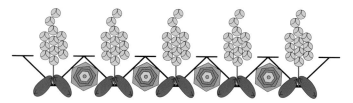

97 **Base-seam template:** Chevron Stitch Base Seam 1; **Thread embroidery stitches:** Chevron Stitch, Straight Stitch, French Knot; **Silk ribbon embroidery stitches:** Straight Stitch; **Beads and baubles:** Seed bead, sequin

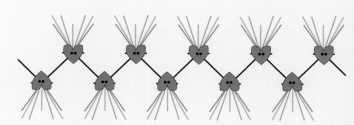

98 **Base-seam template:** Chevron Stitch Base Seam 1; **Thread embroidery stitches:** Chevron Stitch, Straight Stitch; **Silk ribbon embroidery stitches:** None; **Beads and baubles:** Button

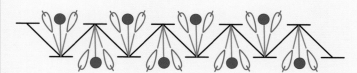

99 **Base-seam template:** Chevron Stitch Base Seam 1; **Thread embroidery stitches:** Chevron Stitch, Straight Stitch, Detached Chain Stitch; **Silk ribbon embroidery stitches:** None; **Beads and baubles:** 3 mm round bead

100 **Base-seam template:** Chevron Stitch Base Seam 1; **Thread embroidery stitches:** Chevron Stitch, Straight Stitch, Detached Chain Stitch, French Knot; **Silk ribbon embroidery stitches:** None; **Beads and baubles:** Seed bead, sequin

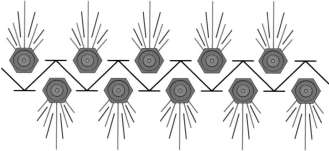

101 **Base-seam template:** Chevron Stitch Base Seam 1; **Thread embroidery stitches:** Chevron Stitch, Straight Stitch; **Silk ribbon embroidery stitches:** None; **Beads and baubles:** Seed bead, sequin

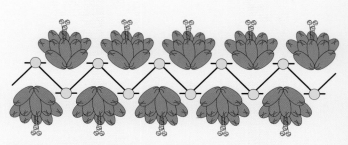

102 **Base-seam template:** Chevron Stitch Base Seam 1; **Thread embroidery stitches:** Chevron Stitch, Straight Stitch, French Knot; **Silk ribbon embroidery stitches:** Straight Stitch; **Beads and baubles:** 3 mm round bead

103 **Base-seam template:** Chevron Stitch Base Seam 1; **Thread embroidery stitches:** Chevron Stitch, Detached Chain Stitch; **Silk ribbon embroidery stitches:** Ribbon Stitch, Fargo Rose; **Beads and baubles:** Button

104 **Base-seam template:** Chevron Stitch Base Seam 1; **Thread embroidery stitches:** Chevron Stitch, Straight Stitch; **Silk ribbon embroidery stitches:** Straight Stitch; **Beads and baubles:** Seed bead, 2 mm round bead, 3 mm round bead, size 15 rocailles

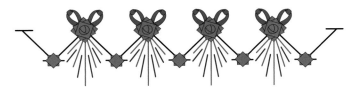

105 **Base-seam template:** Chevron Stitch Base Seam 1; **Thread embroidery stitches:** Chevron Stitch, Straight Stitch; **Silk ribbon embroidery stitches:** Detached Chain Stitch, Fargo Rose; **Beads and baubles:** 4 mm montée

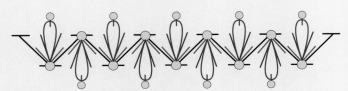

106 **Base-seam template:** Chevron Stitch Base Seam 1; **Thread embroidery stitches:** Chevron Stitch, Straight Stitch, Detached Chain Stitch; **Silk ribbon embroidery stitches:** None; **Beads and baubles:** 3 mm round bead

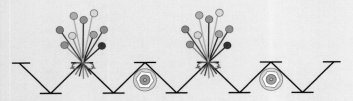

107 **Base-seam template:** Chevron Stitch Base Seam 1; **Thread embroidery stitches:** Chevron Stitch, Detached Chain Stitch, Straight Stitch; **Silk ribbon embroidery stitches:** None; **Beads and baubles:** Seed bead, sequin, 3 mm round bead

108 **Base-seam template:** Chevron Stitch Base Seam 1; **Thread embroidery stitches:** Chevron Stitch, Straight Stitch; **Silk ribbon embroidery stitches:** Straight Stitch, Loop Stitch; **Beads and baubles:** Seed bead, 2 mm round bead, 3 mm round bead, size 15 rocailles

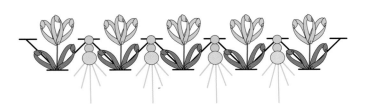

109 **Base-seam template:** Chevron Stitch Base Seam 1; **Thread embroidery stitches:** Chevron Stitch, Straight Stitch; **Silk ribbon embroidery stitches:** Detached Chain Stitch; **Beads and baubles:** 2 mm round bead, 4 mm round bead

110 **Base-seam template:** Chevron Stitch Base Seam 1; **Thread embroidery stitches:** Chevron Stitch, Straight Stitch, Detached Chain Stitch; **Silk ribbon embroidery stitches:** Fargo Rose; **Beads and baubles:** None

111 **Base-seam template:** Chevron Stitch Base Seam 1; **Thread embroidery stitches:** Chevron Stitch, Straight Stitch, Detached Chain Stitch, Bullion Stitch; **Silk ribbon embroidery stitches:** None; **Beads and baubles:** Seed bead, sequin

112 **Base-seam template:** Chevron Stitch Base Seam 1; **Thread embroidery stitches:** Chevron Stitch, Bullion Stitch, French Knot; **Silk ribbon embroidery stitches:** Ribbon Stitch, Fargo Rose; **Beads and baubles:** None

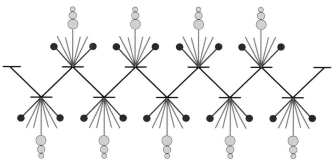

113 **Base-seam template:** Chevron Stitch Base Seam 1; **Thread embroidery stitches:** Chevron Stitch, Straight Stitch; **Silk ribbon embroidery stitches:** None; **Beads and baubles:** Seed bead, 2 mm round bead, 3 mm round bead

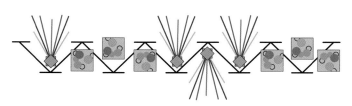

114 **Base-seam template:** Chevron Stitch Base Seam 1; **Thread embroidery stitches:** Chevron Stitch, Detached Chain Stitch, Bullion Stitch; **Silk ribbon embroidery stitches:** None; **Beads and baubles:** Seed bead

115 **Base-seam template:** Chevron Stitch Base Seam 1; **Thread embroidery stitches:** Chevron Stitch, Straight Stitch, French Knot; **Silk ribbon embroidery stitches:** Detached Chain Stitch, Straight Stitch, Fargo Rose; **Beads and baubles:** Rice bead

116 **Base-seam template:** Chevron Stitch Base Seam 1; **Thread embroidery stitches:** Chevron Stitch, Straight Stitch; **Silk ribbon embroidery stitches:** None; **Beads and baubles:** Montée, 6 mm square bead

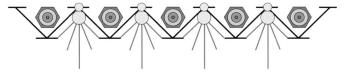

117 **Base-seam template:** Chevron Stitch Base Seam 1; **Thread embroidery stitches:** Chevron Stitch, Straight Stitch; **Silk ribbon embroidery stitches:** None; **Beads and baubles:** Seed bead, 2 mm round bead, 3 mm round bead, sequin

118 **Base-seam template:** Chevron Stitch Base Seam 1; **Thread embroidery stitches:** Chevron Stitch, Straight Stitch; **Silk ribbon embroidery stitches:** Ribbon Stitch, Woven Rose; **Beads and baubles:** Seed bead, sequin

119 **Base-seam template:** Chevron Stitch Base Seam 1; **Thread embroidery stitches:** Chevron Stitch, Detached Chain Stitch, Bullion Stitch; **Silk ribbon embroidery stitches:** None; **Beads and baubles:** 3 mm round bead

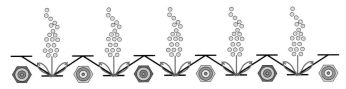

120 **Base-seam template:** Chevron Stitch Base Seam 1; **Thread embroidery stitches:** Chevron Stitch, Straight Stitch, French Knot, Detached Chain Stitch; **Silk ribbon embroidery stitches:** None; **Beads and baubles:** Seed bead, sequin

121 **Base-seam template:** Chevron Stitch Base Seam 1; **Thread embroidery stitches:** Chevron Stitch, Straight Stitch; **Silk ribbon embroidery stitches:** Straight Stitch; **Beads and baubles:** Seed bead, sequin, size 15 rocailles

122 **Base-seam template:** Chevron Stitch Base Seam 1; **Thread embroidery stitches:** Chevron Stitch, Bullion Stitch, Detached Chain Stitch; **Silk ribbon embroidery stitches:** Detached Chain Stitch, Loop Stitch; **Beads and baubles:** 2 mm round bead, 3 mm round bead, 4 mm round bead, 4-hole button

123 **Base-seam template:** Chevron Stitch Base Seam 1; **Thread embroidery stitches:** Chevron Stitch, Straight Stitch, Detached Chain Stitch; **Silk ribbon embroidery stitches:** Detached Chain Stitch; **Beads and baubles:** Seed bead, sequin

124 **Base-seam template:** Chevron Stitch Base Seam 1; **Thread embroidery stitches:** Chevron Stitch, Straight Stitch, Detached Chain Stitch; **Silk ribbon embroidery stitches:** None; **Beads and baubles:** 4 mm round bead

125 **Base-seam template:** Chevron Stitch Base Seam 1; **Thread embroidery stitches:** Chevron Stitch; **Silk ribbon embroidery stitches:** Detached Chain Stitch, Straight Stitch, Ribbon Stitch; **Beads and baubles:** Seed bead, sequin

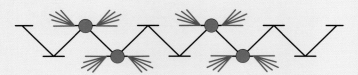

126 **Base-seam template:** Chevron Stitch Base Seam 1; **Thread embroidery stitches:** Chevron Stitch, Straight Stitch; **Silk ribbon embroidery stitches:** None; **Beads and baubles:** 4 mm round bead

127 **Base-seam template:** Chevron Stitch Base Seam 1; **Thread embroidery stitches:** Chevron Stitch, Detached Chain Stitch; **Silk ribbon embroidery stitches:** Straight Stitch, Fargo Rose; **Beads and baubles:** 4 mm montée

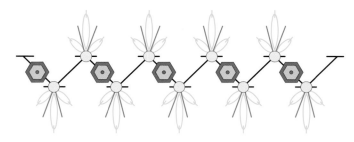

128 **Base-seam template:** Chevron Stitch Base Seam 1; **Thread embroidery stitches:** Chevron Stitch, Detached Chain Stitch, Straight Stitch; **Silk ribbon embroidery stitches:** None; **Beads and baubles:** 3 mm round bead, sequin, seed bead

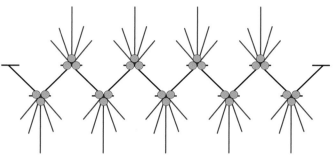

129 **Base-seam template:** Chevron Stitch Base Seam 1; **Thread embroidery stitches:** Chevron Stitch, Straight Stitch; **Silk ribbon embroidery stitches:** None; **Beads and baubles:** 2 mm round bead

130 **Base-seam template:** Chevron Stitch Base Seam 1; **Thread embroidery stitches:** Chevron Stitch, Detached Chain Stitch; **Silk ribbon embroidery stitches:** None; **Beads and baubles:** 2 mm round bead, sequin

131 **Base-seam template:** Chevron Stitch Base Seam 1; **Thread embroidery stitches:** Chevron Stitch; **Silk ribbon embroidery stitches:** Detached Chain Stitch, Woven Rose; **Beads and baubles:** 4 mm montée

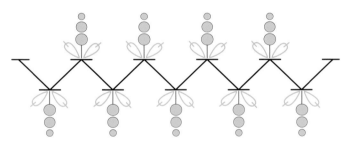

132 **Base-seam template:** Chevron Stitch Base Seam 1; **Thread embroidery stitches:** Chevron Stitch, Detached Chain Stitch, Straight Stitch; **Silk ribbon embroidery stitches:** None; **Beads and baubles:** 2 mm round bead, 3 mm round bead, 4 mm round bead

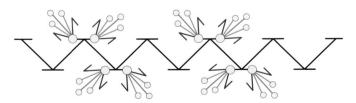

133 **Base-seam template:** Chevron Stitch Base Seam 1; **Thread embroidery stitches:** Chevron Stitch, Straight Stitch; **Silk ribbon embroidery stitches:** None; **Beads and baubles:** Seed bead, 2 mm round bead

134 **Base-seam template:** Chevron Stitch Base Seam 1; **Thread embroidery stitches:** Chevron Stitch, Straight Stitch; **Silk ribbon embroidery stitches:** Straight Stitch, Detached Chain Stitch; **Beads and baubles:** Seed bead, 3 mm round bead, sequin

135 **Base-seam template:** Chevron Stitch Base Seam 1; **Thread embroidery stitches:** Chevron Stitch, Detached Chain Stitch, Straight Stitch; **Silk ribbon embroidery stitches:** Straight Stitch; **Beads and baubles:** 3 mm round bead

136 **Base-seam template:** Chevron Stitch Base Seam 1; **Thread embroidery stitches:** Chevron Stitch, Detached Chain Stitch, Straight Stitch; **Silk ribbon embroidery stitches:** Fargo Rose; **Beads and baubles:** None

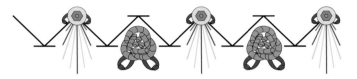

137 **Base-seam template:** Chevron Stitch Base Seam 1; **Thread embroidery stitches:** Chevron Stitch, Bullion Stitch, Straight Stitch, French Knot; **Silk ribbon embroidery stitches:** Detached Chain Stitch; **Beads and baubles:** Seed bead, sequin

138 **Base-seam template:** Chevron Stitch Base Seam 1; **Thread embroidery stitches:** Chevron Stitch, Straight Stitch; **Silk ribbon embroidery stitches:** Straight Stitch; **Beads and baubles:** Seed bead, sequin, size 15 rocailles

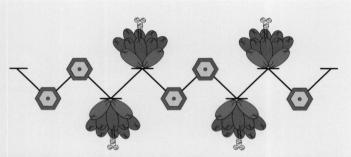

139 **Base-seam template:** Chevron Stitch Base Seam 1; **Thread embroidery stitches:** Chevron Stitch, French Knot, Straight Stitch; **Silk ribbon embroidery stitches:** Straight Stitch; **Beads and baubles:** Seed bead, sequin

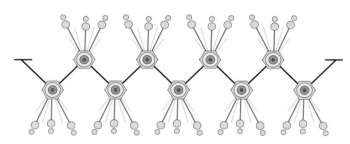

140 **Base-seam template:** Chevron Stitch Base Seam 1; **Thread embroidery stitches:** Chevron Stitch, Straight Stitch; **Silk ribbon embroidery stitches:** None; **Beads and baubles:** Seed bead, 2 mm round bead, sequin

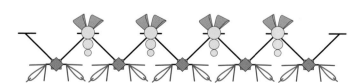

141 **Base-seam template:** Chevron Stitch Base Seam 1; **Thread embroidery stitches:** Chevron Stitch, Detached Chain Stitch, Straight Stitch; **Silk ribbon embroidery stitches:** Loop Stitch; **Beads and baubles:** 2 mm round bead, 3 mm round bead, 4 mm round bead, 4 mm montée

142 **Base-seam template:** Chevron Stitch Base Seam 2; **Thread embroidery stitches:** Chevron Stitch, Detached Chain Stitch, Straight Stitch, Bullion Stitch; **Silk ribbon embroidery stitches:** None; **Beads and baubles:** 2 mm round bead, 4 mm round bead, sequin

143 **Base-seam template:** Chevron Stitch Base Seam 2; **Thread embroidery stitches:** Chevron Stitch, Bullion Stitch; **Silk ribbon embroidery stitches:** Ribbon Stitch; **Beads and baubles:** 2 mm round bead

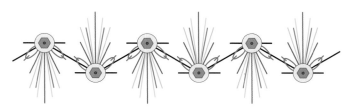

144 **Base-seam template:** Chevron Stitch Base Seam 2; **Thread embroidery stitches:** Chevron Stitch, Detached Chain Stitch, Straight Stitch; **Silk ribbon embroidery stitches:** None; **Beads and baubles:** Seed bead, sequin

145 **Base-seam template:** Chevron Stitch Base Seam 2; **Thread embroidery stitches:** Chevron Stitch; **Silk ribbon embroidery stitches:** Straight Stitch, Stem Stitch Rose; **Beads and baubles:** Seed bead, sequin

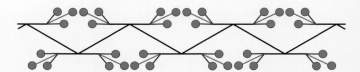

146 **Base-seam template:** Chevron Stitch Base Seam 2; **Thread embroidery stitches:** Chevron Stitch, Straight Stitch; **Silk ribbon embroidery stitches:** None; **Beads and baubles:** 2 mm round bead

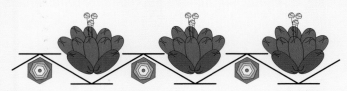

147 **Base-seam template:** Chevron Stitch Base Seam 2; **Thread embroidery stitches:** Chevron Stitch, French Knot, Straight Stitch; **Silk ribbon embroidery stitches:** Straight Stitch; **Beads and baubles:** Seed bead, sequin

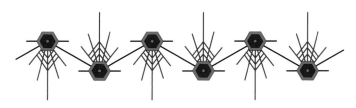

148 **Base-seam template:** Chevron Stitch Base Seam 2; **Thread embroidery stitches:** Chevron Stitch, Straight Stitch; **Silk ribbon embroidery stitches:** None; **Beads and baubles:** Seed bead, sequin

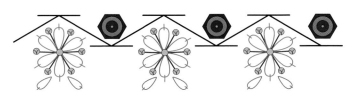

149 **Base-seam template:** Chevron Stitch Base Seam 2; **Thread embroidery stitches:** Chevron Stitch, Detached Chain Stitch, Straight Stitch, French Knot; **Silk ribbon embroidery stitches:** None; **Beads and baubles:** Seed bead, sequin

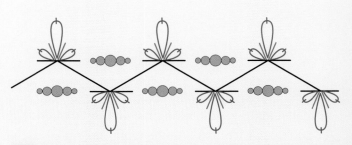

150 **Base-seam template:** Chevron Stitch Base Seam 2; **Thread embroidery stitches:** Chevron Stitch, Detached Chain Stitch, Straight Stitch; **Silk ribbon embroidery stitches:** None; **Beads and baubles:** Seed bead, 2 mm round bead, 3 mm round bead

151 **Base-seam template:** Chevron Stitch Base Seam 2; **Thread embroidery stitches:** Chevron Stitch, Straight Stitch; **Silk ribbon embroidery stitches:** Straight Stitch; **Beads and baubles:** 3 mm montée, size 15 rocailles

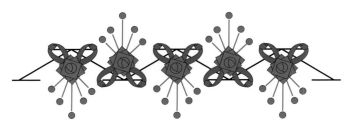

152 **Base-seam template:** Chevron Stitch Base Seam 2; **Thread embroidery stitches:** Chevron Stitch, Straight Stitch; **Silk ribbon embroidery stitches:** Detached Chain Stitch, Fargo Rose; **Beads and baubles:** 2 mm round bead

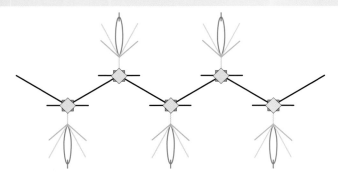

153 **Base-seam template:** Chevron Stitch Base Seam 2; **Thread embroidery stitches:** Chevron Stitch, Detached Chain Stitch, Straight Stitch; **Silk ribbon embroidery stitches:** None; **Beads and baubles:** 4 mm montée

154 **Base-seam template:** Chevron Stitch Base Seam 2; **Thread embroidery stitches:** Chevron Stitch, Straight Stitch; **Silk ribbon embroidery stitches:** Detached Chain Stitch; **Beads and baubles:** 2 mm round bead, 4 mm round bead, 3 mm montée

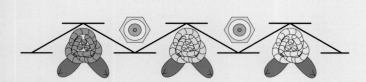

155 **Base-seam template:** Chevron Stitch Base Seam 2; **Thread embroidery stitches:** Chevron Stitch, Bullion Stitch, French Knot; **Silk ribbon embroidery stitches:** Straight Stitch; **Beads and baubles:** Seed bead, sequin

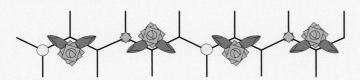

156 **Base-seam template:** Cretan Stitch Base Seam 1; **Thread embroidery stitches:** Cretan Stitch; **Silk ribbon embroidery stitches:** Ribbon Stitch, Fargo Rose; **Beads and baubles:** 3 mm round bead, 2 mm montée

157 **Base-seam template:** Cretan Stitch Base Seam 1; **Thread embroidery stitches:** Cretan Stitch; **Silk ribbon embroidery stitches:** Loop Stitch; **Beads and baubles:** 2 mm round bead, 3 mm round bead, 4 mm round bead

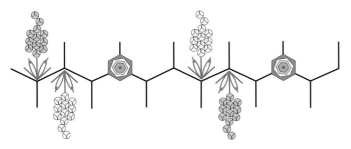

158 **Base-seam template:** Cretan Stitch Base Seam 1; **Thread embroidery stitches:** Cretan Stitch, Detached Chain Stitch, Straight Stitch, French Knot; **Silk ribbon embroidery stitches:** None; **Beads and baubles:** Seed bead, sequin

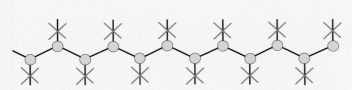

159 **Base-seam template:** Cretan Stitch Base Seam 1; **Thread embroidery stitches:** Cretan Stitch; **Silk ribbon embroidery stitches:** Ribbon Stitch, Straight Stitch, Detached Chain Stitch, **Beads and baubles:** Seed bead, sequin

160 **Base-seam template:** Cretan Stitch Base Seam 1; **Thread embroidery stitches:** Cretan Stitch, Straight Stitch; **Silk ribbon embroidery stitches:** None; **Beads and baubles:** 3 mm round bead

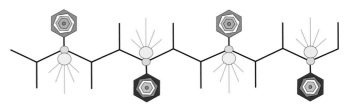

161 **Base-seam template:** Cretan Stitch Base Seam 1; **Thread embroidery stitches:** Cretan Stitch, Straight Stitch; **Silk ribbon embroidery stitches:** None; **Beads and baubles:** 2 mm round bead, 3 mm round bead, seed bead, sequin

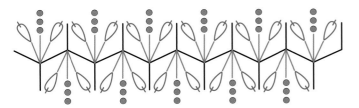

162 **Base-seam template:** Cretan Stitch Base Seam 1; **Thread embroidery stitches:** Cretan Stitch, Detached Chain Stitch, Straight Stitch; **Silk ribbon embroidery stitches:** None; **Beads and baubles:** 2 mm round bead

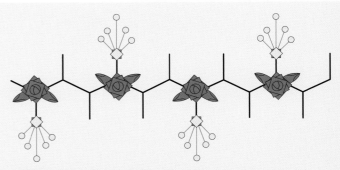

163 **Base-seam template:** Cretan Stitch Base Seam 1; **Thread embroidery stitches:** Cretan Stitch, Straight Stitch; **Silk ribbon embroidery stitches:** Ribbon Stitch, Fargo Roses; **Beads and baubles:** 2 mm round bead, 3 mm montée

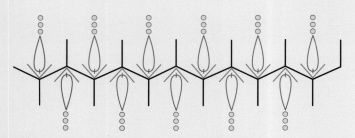

164 **Base-seam template:** Cretan Stitch Base Seam 1; **Thread embroidery stitches:** Cretan Stitch, Detached Chain Stitch, Straight Stitch; **Silk ribbon embroidery stitches:** None; **Beads and baubles:** Seed bead

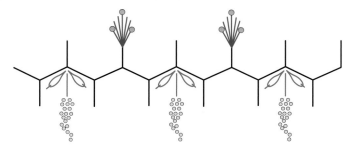

165 **Base-seam template:** Cretan Stitch Base Seam 1; **Thread embroidery stitches:** Cretan Stitch, French Knot, Detached Chain Stitch, Straight Stitch; **Silk ribbon embroidery stitches:** None; **Beads and baubles:** 2 mm round bead

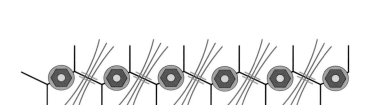

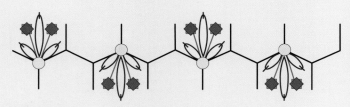

166 **Base-seam template:** Cretan Stitch Base Seam 1; **Thread embroidery stitches:** Cretan Stitch, Straight Stitch; **Silk ribbon embroidery stitches:** None; **Beads and baubles:** 2 mm round bead, sequin

167 **Base-seam template:** Cretan Stitch Base Seam 1; **Thread embroidery stitches:** Cretan Stitch, Detached Chain Stitch, Straight Stitch; **Silk ribbon embroidery stitches:** None; **Beads and baubles:** 4 mm round bead, 4 mm montée

168 **Base-seam template:** Cretan Stitch Base Seam 1; **Thread embroidery stitches:** Cretan Stitch, Detached Chain Stitch, Straight Stitch; **Silk ribbon embroidery stitches:** None; **Beads and baubles:** 2 mm round bead

169 **Base-seam template:** Cretan Stitch Base Seam 1; **Thread embroidery stitches:** Cretan Stitch, Detached Chain Stitch, Bullion Stitch, Straight Stitch; **Silk ribbon embroidery stitches:** None; **Beads and baubles:** 2 mm round bead, 3 mm round bead, seed bead

170 **Base-seam template:** Cretan Stitch Base Seam 1; **Thread embroidery stitches:** Cretan Stitch, Detached Chain Stitch, Straight Stitch; **Silk ribbon embroidery stitches:** None; **Beads and baubles:** 2 mm round bead, seed bead, sequin

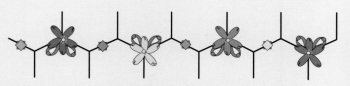

171 **Base-seam template:** Cretan Stitch Base Seam 1; **Thread embroidery stitches:** Cretan Stitch, Straight Stitch; **Silk ribbon embroidery stitches:** Straight Stitch, Detached Chain Stitch; **Beads and baubles:** Seed bead, 2 mm montée

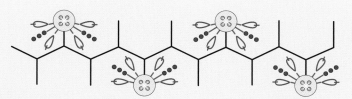

172 **Base-seam template:** Cretan Stitch Base Seam 1; **Thread embroidery stitches:** Cretan Stitch, Detached Chain Stitch, Straight Stitch; **Silk ribbon embroidery stitches:** None; **Beads and baubles:** Seed bead, button

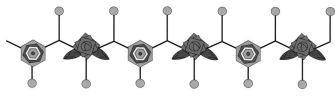

173 **Base-seam template:** Cretan Stitch Base Seam 1; **Thread embroidery stitches:** Cretan Stitch; **Silk ribbon embroidery stitches:** Ribbon Stitch, Fargo Rose; **Beads and baubles:** 2 mm round bead, seed bead, sequin

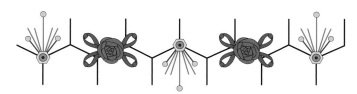

174 **Base-seam template:** Cretan Stitch Base Seam 1; **Thread embroidery stitches:** Cretan Stitch, Straight Stitch; **Silk ribbon embroidery stitches:** Detached Chain Stitch, Woven Rose; **Beads and baubles:** Seed bead, sequin

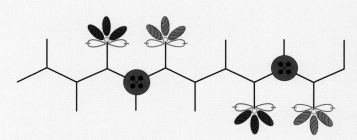

175 **Base-seam template:** Cretan Stitch Base Seam 1; **Thread embroidery stitches:** Cretan Stitch, Detached Chain Stitch, Bullion Stitch; **Silk ribbon embroidery stitches:** None; **Beads and baubles:** Seed bead, button

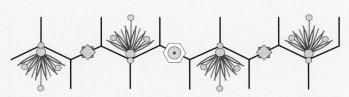

176 **Base-seam template:** Cretan Stitch Base Seam 1; **Thread embroidery stitches:** Cretan Stitch, Detached Chain Stitch, Straight Stitch; **Silk ribbon embroidery stitches:** None; **Beads and baubles:** 2 mm round bead, seed bead, 3 mm montée, sequin

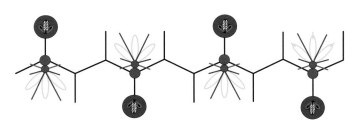

177 **Base-seam template:** Cretan Stitch Base Seam 1; **Thread embroidery stitches:** Cretan Stitch, Detached Chain Stitch, Bullion Stitch, Straight Stitch; **Silk ribbon embroidery stitches:** None; **Beads and baubles:** 2 mm round bead, 3 mm round bead, button

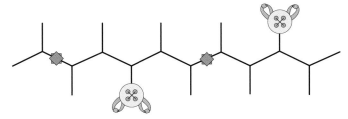

178 **Base-seam template:** Cretan Stitch Base Seam 1; **Thread embroidery stitches:** Cretan Stitch; **Silk ribbon embroidery stitches:** Detached Chain Stitch; **Beads and baubles:** 3 mm montée, button

179 **Base-seam template:** Cretan Stitch Base Seam 1; **Thread embroidery stitches:** Cretan Stitch; **Silk ribbon embroidery stitches:** Detached Chain Stitch; **Beads and baubles:** 3 mm round bead

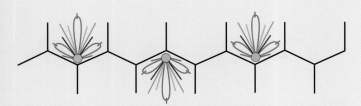

180 **Base-seam template:** Cretan Stitch Base Seam 1; **Thread embroidery stitches:** Cretan Stitch, Detached Chain Stitch, Straight Stitch; **Silk ribbon embroidery stitches:** None; **Beads and baubles:** 3 mm round bead

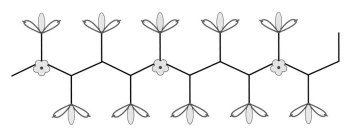

181 **Base-seam template:** Cretan Stitch Base Seam 1; **Thread embroidery stitches:** Cretan Stitch, Detached Chain Stitch; **Silk ribbon embroidery stitches:** None; **Beads and baubles:** Rice bead, flower cap bead, seed bead

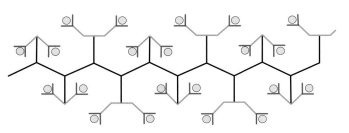

182 **Base-seam template:** Cretan Stitch Base Seam 1; **Thread embroidery stitches:** Cretan Stitch, Straight Stitch; **Silk ribbon embroidery stitches:** None; **Beads and baubles:** 2 mm round bead

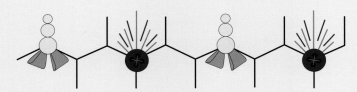

183 **Base-seam template:** Cretan Stitch Base Seam 1; **Thread embroidery stitches:** Cretan Stitch, Straight Stitch; **Silk ribbon embroidery stitches:** Loop Stitch; **Beads and baubles:** 2 mm round bead, 3 mm round bead, 4 mm round bead, button

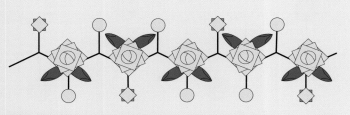

184 **Base-seam template:** Cretan Stitch Base Seam 1; **Thread embroidery stitches:** Cretan Stitch; **Silk ribbon embroidery stitches:** Ribbon Stitch, Fargo Rose; **Beads and baubles:** 3 mm round bead, 3 mm montée

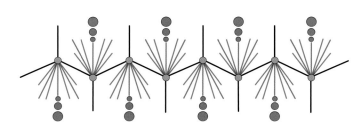

185 **Base-seam template:** Cretan Stitch Base Seam 1; **Thread embroidery stitches:** Cretan Stitch, Straight Stitch; **Silk ribbon embroidery stitches:** None; **Beads and baubles:** 2 mm round bead, 3 mm round bead, seed bead

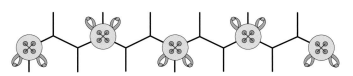

186 **Base-seam template:** Cretan Stitch Base Seam 1; **Thread embroidery stitches:** Cretan Stitch; **Silk ribbon embroidery stitches:** Detached Chain Stitch; **Beads and baubles:** Button

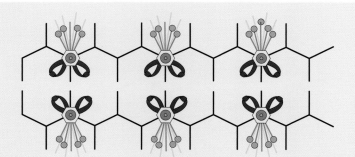

187 **Base-seam template:** Cretan Stitch Base Seam 1; **Thread embroidery stitches:** Cretan Stitch, Straight Stitch; **Silk ribbon embroidery stitches:** Detached Chain Stitch; **Beads and baubles:** 2 mm round bead, seed bead, sequin

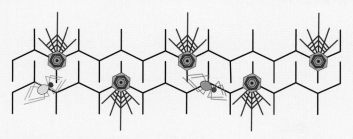

188 **Base-seam template:** Cretan Stitch Base Seam 2; **Thread embroidery stitches:** Cretan Stitch, Straight Stitch; **Silk ribbon embroidery stitches:** None; **Beads and baubles:** Seed bead, 3 mm round bead, sequin

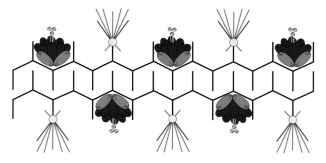

189 **Base-seam template:** Cretan Stitch Base Seam 2; **Thread embroidery stitches:** Cretan Stitch, French Knot, Straight Stitch; **Silk ribbon embroidery stitches:** Straight Stitch; **Beads and baubles:** 2 mm round bead

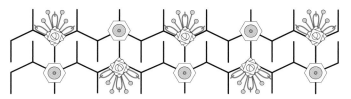

190 **Base-seam template:** Cretan Stitch Base Seam 2; **Thread embroidery stitches:** Cretan Stitch, Detached Chain Stitch, Straight Stitch; **Silk ribbon embroidery stitches:** Fargo Rose; **Beads and baubles:** 2 mm round bead, seed bead, sequin

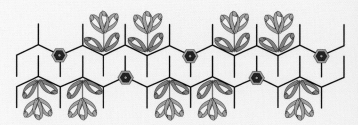

191 **Base-seam template:** Cretan Stitch Base Seam 2; **Thread embroidery stitches:** Cretan Stitch, Straight Stitch; **Silk ribbon embroidery stitches:** Detached Chain Stitch; **Beads and baubles:** Seed bead, sequin

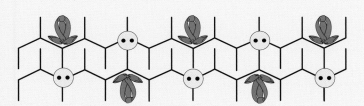

192 **Base-seam template:** Cretan Stitch Base Seam 2; **Thread embroidery stitches:** Cretan Stitch; **Silk ribbon embroidery stitches:** Ribbon Stitch, Straight Stitch, Detached Chain Stitch; **Beads and baubles:** Button

193 **Base-seam template:** Cretan Stitch Base Seam 2; **Thread embroidery stitches:** Cretan Stitch, French Knot, Straight Stitch; **Silk ribbon embroidery stitches:** Ribbon Stitch, Detached Chain Stitch, Woven Rose; **Beads and baubles:** None

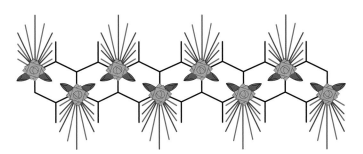

194 **Base-seam template:** Cretan Stitch Base Seam 3; **Thread embroidery stitches:** Cretan Stitch, Straight Stitch; **Silk ribbon embroidery stitches:** Ribbon Stitch, Fargo Rose; **Beads and baubles:** None

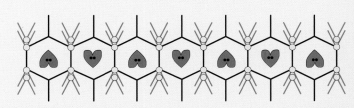

195 **Base-seam template:** Cretan Stitch Base Seam 3 **Thread embroidery stitches:** Cretan Stitch, Straight Stitch; **Silk ribbon embroidery stitches:** None; **Beads and baubles:** Seed bead, heart button

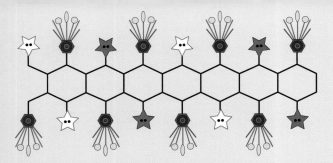

196 **Base-seam template:** Cretan Stitch Base Seam 3; **Thread embroidery stitches:** Cretan Stitch, Straight Stitch; **Silk ribbon embroidery stitches:** None; **Beads and baubles:** 2 mm round bead, rice bead, seed bead, sequin, star button

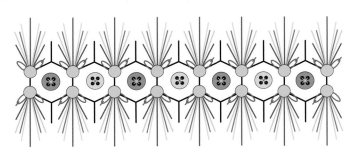

197 **Base-seam template:** Cretan Stitch Base Seam 3; **Thread embroidery stitches:** Cretan Stitch, Detached Chain Stitch, Straight Stitch; **Silk ribbon embroidery stitches:** None; **Beads and baubles:** Button, 4 mm round bead

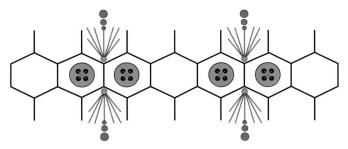

198 **Base-seam template:** Cretan Stitch Base Seam 3; **Thread embroidery stitches:** Cretan Stitch, Straight Stitch; **Silk ribbon embroidery stitches:** None; **Beads and baubles:** 2 mm round bead, 3 mm round bead, seed bead, button

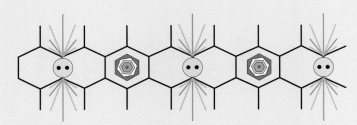

199 **Base-seam template:** Cretan Stitch Base Seam 3; **Thread embroidery stitches:** Cretan Stitch, Straight Stitch; **Silk ribbon embroidery stitches:** None; **Beads and baubles:** Seed bead, sequin, button

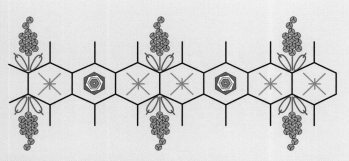

200 **Base-seam template:** Cretan Stitch Base Seam 3; **Thread embroidery stitches:** Cretan Stitch, Detached Chain Stitch, French Knot, Straight Stitch; **Silk ribbon embroidery stitches:** None; **Beads and baubles:** Seed bead, sequin

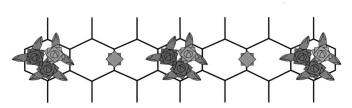

201 **Base-seam template:** Cretan Stitch Base Seam 3; **Thread embroidery stitches:** Cretan Stitch; **Silk ribbon embroidery stitches:** Ribbon Stitch, Fargo Rose; **Beads and baubles:** 4 mm montée

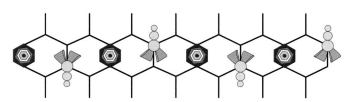

202 **Base-seam template:** Cretan Stitch Base Seam 3; **Thread embroidery stitches:** Cretan Stitch; **Silk ribbon embroidery stitches:** Loop Stitch; **Beads and baubles:** Seed bead, sequin, 3 mm round bead, 2 mm round bead

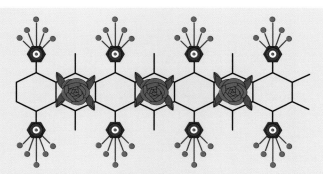

203 **Base-seam template:** Cretan Stitch Base Seam 3; **Thread embroidery stitches:** Cretan Stitch, Straight Stitch; **Silk ribbon embroidery stitches:** Ribbon Stitch, Woven Rose; **Beads and baubles:** Seed bead, sequin, 2 mm round bead

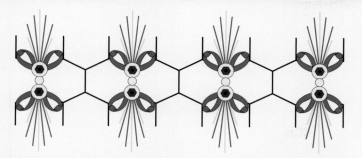

204 **Base-seam template:** Cretan Stitch Base Seam 3; **Thread embroidery stitches:** Cretan Stitch, Straight Stitch; **Silk ribbon embroidery stitches:** Detached Chain Stitch; **Beads and baubles:** 3 mm round bead, seed bead, sequin

205 **Base-seam template:** Cretan Stitch Base Seam 3; **Thread embroidery stitches:** Cretan Stitch, Detached Chain Stitch, Straight Stitch, Back Stitch; **Silk ribbon embroidery stitches:** None; **Beads and baubles:** 3 mm round bead, 4 mm round bead

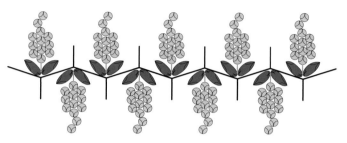

206 **Base-seam template:** Cretan Stitch Base Seam 4; **Thread embroidery stitches:** Cretan Stitch, Straight Stitch, French Knot; **Silk ribbon embroidery stitches:** Ribbon Stitch; **Beads and baubles:** None

207 **Base-seam template:** Cretan Stitch Base Seam 4; **Thread embroidery stitches:** Cretan Stitch, Detached Chain Stitch, Straight Stitch; **Silk ribbon embroidery stitches:** Straight Stitch, Detached Chain Stitch; **Beads and baubles:** Seed bead

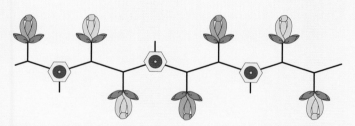

208 **Base-seam template:** Cretan Stitch Base Seam 4; **Thread embroidery stitches:** Cretan Stitch; **Silk ribbon embroidery stitches:** Ribbon Stitch, Straight Stitch, Detached Chain Stitch; **Beads and baubles:** Seed bead, sequin

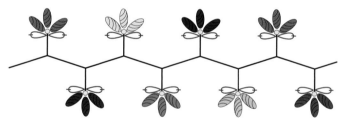

209 **Base-seam template:** Cretan Stitch Base Seam 4; **Thread embroidery stitches:** Cretan Stitch, Detached Chain Stitch, Bullion Stitch; **Silk ribbon embroidery stitches:** None; **Beads and baubles:** Seed bead

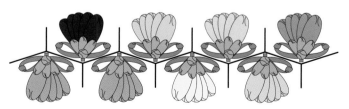

210 **Base-seam template:** Cretan Stitch Base Seam 4; **Thread embroidery stitches:** Cretan Stitch; **Silk ribbon embroidery stitches:** Straight Stitch, French Knot, Detached Chain Stitch; **Beads and baubles:** None

211 **Base-seam template:** Cretan Stitch Base Seam 4; **Thread embroidery stitches:** Cretan Stitch, Detached Chain Stitch (Note that the Detached Chain Stitches used here have a wider base; A and B are set farther apart than usual.); **Silk ribbon embroidery stitches:** Detached Chain Stitch, Fargo Rose; **Beads and baubles:** None

212 Base-seam template: Cretan Stitch Base Seam 4; **Thread embroidery stitches:** Cretan Stitch; **Silk ribbon embroidery stitches:** Detached Chain Stitch, French Knot, Stem Stitch Rose; **Beads and baubles:** 2 mm montée

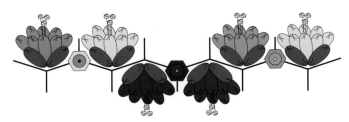

213 Base-seam template: Cretan Stitch Base Seam 4; **Thread embroidery stitches:** Cretan Stitch, French Knot, Straight Stitch; **Silk ribbon embroidery stitches:** Straight Stitch; **Beads and baubles:** Seed bead, sequin

214 Base-seam template: Cretan Stitch Base Seam 4; **Thread embroidery stitches:** Cretan Stitch, Detached Chain Stitch, French Knot, Straight Stitch; **Silk ribbon embroidery stitches:** None; **Beads and baubles:** None

215 Base-seam template: Cretan Stitch Base Seam 4; **Thread embroidery stitches:** Cretan Stitch, Detached Chain Stitch, Straight Stitch; **Silk ribbon embroidery stitches:** None; **Beads and baubles:** Seed bead, sequin

216 Base-seam template: Cretan Stitch Base Seam 4; **Thread embroidery stitches:** Cretan Stitch, Straight Stitch; **Silk ribbon embroidery stitches:** None; **Beads and baubles:** None

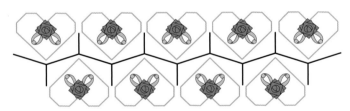

217 Base-seam template: Cretan Stitch Base Seam 4; **Thread embroidery stitches:** Cretan Stitch, Straight Stitch; **Silk ribbon embroidery stitches:** Detached Chain Stitch, Fargo Rose; **Beads and baubles:** None

218 **Base-seam template:** Feather Stitch Base Seam 1; **Thread embroidery stitches:** Feather Stitch, French Knot, Straight Stitch; **Silk ribbon embroidery stitches:** Straight Stitch, Detached Chain Stitch; **Beads and baubles:** 3 mm round bead

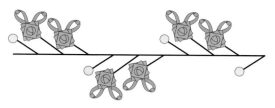

219 **Base-seam template:** Feather Stitch Base Seam 1; **Thread embroidery stitches:** Feather Stitch; **Silk ribbon embroidery stitches:** Detached Chain Stitch, Fargo Rose; **Beads and baubles:** 4 mm round bead

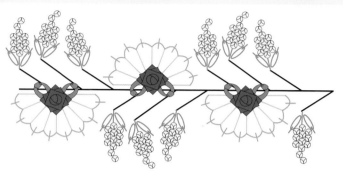

220 **Base-seam template:** Feather Stitch Base Seam 1; **Thread embroidery stitches:** Feather Stitch, French Knot, Detached Chain Stitch, Straight Stitch; **Silk ribbon embroidery stitches:** Detached Chain Stitch, Fargo Rose; **Beads and baubles:** None

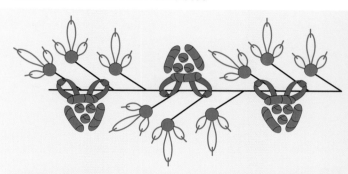

221 **Base-seam template:** Feather Stitch Base Seam 1; **Thread embroidery stitches:** Feather Stitch, Detached Chain Stitch; **Silk ribbon embroidery stitches:** Detached Chain Stitch, French Knot, Wrapped Straight Stitch; **Beads and baubles:** 4 mm round bead

222 **Base-seam template:** Feather Stitch Base Seam 1; **Thread embroidery stitches:** Feather Stitch, Detached Chain Stitch, Straight Stitch; **Silk ribbon embroidery stitches:** Ribbon Stitch, French Knot, Stem Stitch Rose; **Beads and baubles:** 2 mm round bead, 3 mm round bead, 4 mm round bead

223 **Base-seam template:** Feather Stitch Base Seam 1; **Thread embroidery stitches:** Feather Stitch, Bullion Stitch, Detached Chain Stitch, Straight Stitch; **Silk ribbon embroidery stitches:** None; **Beads and baubles:** Seed bead, sequin, 3 mm round bead

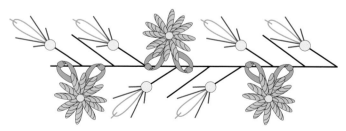

224 **Base-seam template:** Feather Stitch Base Seam 1; **Thread embroidery stitches:** Feather Stitch, Bullion Stitch, Detached Chain Stitch, Straight Stitch; **Silk ribbon embroidery stitches:** Detached Chain Stitch; **Beads and baubles:** Seed bead, 4 mm round bead

225 **Base-seam template:** Feather Stitch Base Seam 1; **Thread embroidery stitches:** Feather Stitch, Detached Chain Stitch, Straight Stitch; **Silk ribbon embroidery stitches:** Straight Stitch; **Beads and baubles:** 3 mm round bead, size 15 rocailles

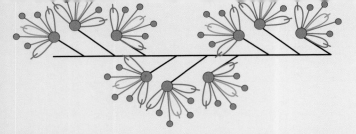

226 **Base-seam template:** Feather Stitch Base Seam 1; **Thread embroidery stitches:** Feather Stitch, Detached Chain Stitch, Straight Stitch; **Silk ribbon embroidery stitches:** None; **Beads and baubles:** 2 mm round bead, 4 mm round bead

227 **Base-seam template:** Feather Stitch Base Seam 1; **Thread embroidery stitches:** Feather Stitch, Straight Stitch, Detached Chain Stitch; **Silk ribbon embroidery stitches:** Ribbon Stitch, Fargo Rose; **Beads and baubles:** 4 mm round bead

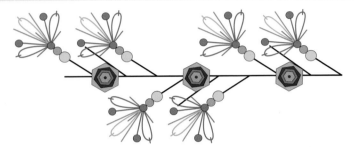

228 **Base-seam template:** Feather Stitch Base Seam 1; **Thread embroidery stitches:** Feather Stitch, Straight Stitch, Detached Chain Stitch; **Silk ribbon embroidery stitches:** None; **Beads and baubles:** 2 mm round bead, 3 mm round bead, 4 mm round bead, seed bead, sequin

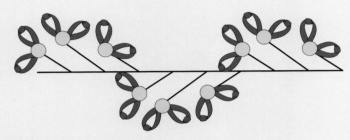

229 **Base-seam template:** Feather Stitch Base Seam 1; **Thread embroidery stitches:** Feather Stitch; **Silk ribbon embroidery stitches:** Detached Chain Stitch; **Beads and baubles:** 4 mm round bead

230 **Base-seam template:** Feather Stitch Base Seam 1; **Thread embroidery stitches:** Feather Stitch, Straight Stitch; **Silk ribbon embroidery stitches:** Straight Stitch, Detached Chain Stitch; **Beads and baubles:** 3 mm round bead, seed bead, sequin

231 **Base-seam template:** Feather Stitch Base Seam 1; **Thread embroidery stitches:** Feather Stitch, Straight Stitch; **Silk ribbon embroidery stitches:** Detached Chain Stitch, Straight Stitch; **Beads and baubles:** Seed bead, 4 mm montée

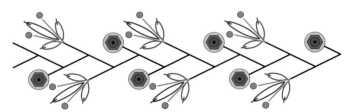

232 **Base-seam template:** Feather Stitch Base Seam 2; **Thread embroidery stitches:** Feather Stitch, Detached Chain Stitch, Straight Stitch; **Silk ribbon embroidery stitches:** None; **Beads and baubles:** 2 mm round bead, seed bead, sequin

233 **Base-seam template:** Feather Stitch Base Seam 2; **Thread embroidery stitches:** Feather Stitch, Straight Stitch; **Silk ribbon embroidery stitches:** None; **Beads and baubles:** Seed bead

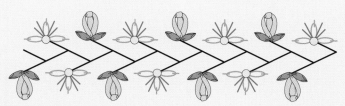

234 **Base-seam template:** Feather Stitch Base Seam 2; **Thread embroidery stitches:** Feather Stitch, Detached Chain Stitch, Straight Stitch; **Silk ribbon embroidery stitches:** Ribbon Stitch, Straight Stitch, Detached Chain Stitch; **Beads and baubles:** 3 mm round bead

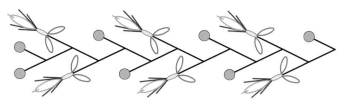

235 **Base-seam template:** Feather Stitch Base Seam 2; **Thread embroidery stitches:** Feather Stitch, Detached Chain Stitch, Straight Stitch; **Silk ribbon embroidery stitches:** None; **Beads and baubles:** 2 mm round bead, rice bead

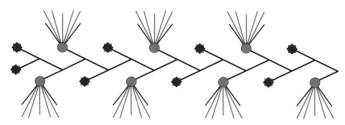

236 **Base-seam template:** Feather Stitch Base Seam 2; **Thread embroidery stitches:** Feather Stitch, Straight Stitch; **Silk ribbon embroidery stitches:** None; **Beads and baubles:** 2 mm round bead, 2 mm montée

237 **Base-seam template:** Feather Stitch Base Seam 2; **Thread embroidery stitches:** Feather Stitch; **Silk ribbon embroidery stitches:** Detached Chain Stitch, Fargo Rose; **Beads and baubles:** 2 mm round bead, 3 mm round bead, seed bead

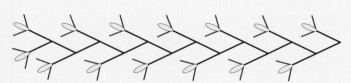

238 **Base-seam template:** Feather Stitch Base Seam 2; **Thread embroidery stitches:** Feather Stitch, Straight Stitch; **Silk ribbon embroidery stitches:** None; **Beads and baubles:** Rice bead

239 **Base-seam template:** Feather Stitch Base Seam 2; **Thread embroidery stitches:** Feather Stitch, Detached Chain Stitch; **Silk ribbon embroidery stitches:** None; **Beads and baubles:** 4 mm montée

240 **Base-seam template:** Feather Stitch Base Seam 2 **Thread embroidery stitches:** Feather Stitch, Detached Chain Stitch, Straight Stitch; **Silk ribbon embroidery stitches:** None; **Beads and baubles:** 2 mm round bead, 3 mm round bead, seed bead

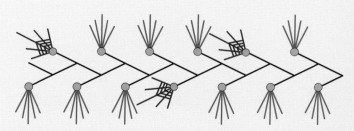

241 **Base-seam template:** Feather Stitch Base Seam 2; **Thread embroidery stitches:** Feather Stitch, Straight Stitch; **Silk ribbon embroidery stitches:** None; **Beads and baubles:** 2 mm round bead

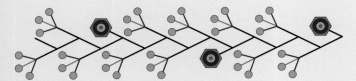

242 **Base-seam template:** Feather Stitch Base Seam 2; **Thread embroidery stitches:** Feather Stitch, Straight Stitch; **Silk ribbon embroidery stitches:** None; **Beads and baubles:** 2 mm round bead, seed bead, sequin

243 **Base-seam template:** Feather Stitch Base Seam 2; **Thread embroidery stitches:** Feather Stitch, Detached Chain Stitch, Bullion Stitch; **Silk ribbon embroidery stitches:** None; **Beads and baubles:** Seed bead

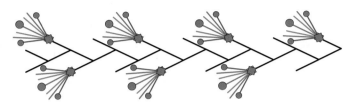

244 **Base-seam template:** Feather Stitch Base Seam 2; **Thread embroidery stitches:** Feather Stitch, Straight Stitch; **Silk ribbon embroidery stitches:** None; **Beads and baubles:** 2 mm round bead, 2 mm montée, seed bead

245 **Base-seam template:** Feather Stitch Base Seam 2; **Thread embroidery stitches:** Feather Stitch, Detached Chain Stitch, Straight Stitch; **Silk ribbon embroidery stitches:** None; **Beads and baubles:** None

246 **Base-seam template:** Feather Stitch Base Seam 2; **Thread embroidery stitches:** Feather Stitch, Detached Chain Stitch, Straight Stitch; **Silk ribbon embroidery stitches:** None; **Beads and baubles:** 3 mm montée

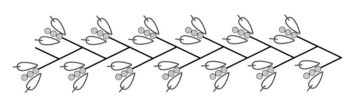

247 **Base-seam template:** Feather Stitch Base Seam 2; **Thread embroidery stitches:** Feather Stitch, Detached Chain Stitch; **Silk ribbon embroidery stitches:** None; **Beads and baubles:** 2 mm round bead

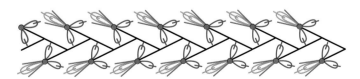

248 **Base-seam template:** Feather Stitch Base Seam 2; **Thread embroidery stitches:** Feather Stitch, Detached Chain Stitch, Straight Stitch; **Silk ribbon embroidery stitches:** None; **Beads and baubles:** Seed bead

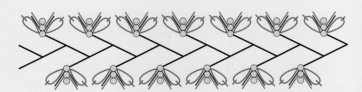

249 **Base-seam template:** Feather Stitch Base Seam 2; **Thread embroidery stitches:** Feather Stitch, Detached Chain Stitch, Straight Stitch; **Silk ribbon embroidery stitches:** None; **Beads and baubles:** Seed bead

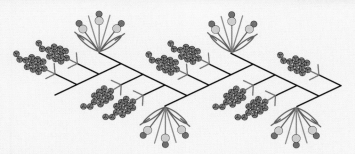

250 **Base-seam template:** Feather Stitch Base Seam 3; **Thread embroidery stitches:** Feather Stitch, Detached Chain Stitch, French Knot, Straight Stitch; **Silk ribbon embroidery stitches:** None; **Beads and baubles:** 2 mm round bead, 3 mm round bead

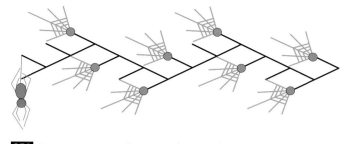

251 **Base-seam template:** Feather Stitch Base Seam 3; **Thread embroidery stitches:** Feather Stitch, Straight Stitch; **Silk ribbon embroidery stitches:** None; **Beads and baubles:** 2 mm round bead, 3 mm round bead, oval bead

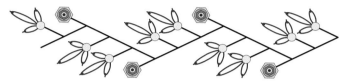

252 **Base-seam template:** Feather Stitch Base Seam 3; **Thread embroidery stitches:** Feather Stitch, Detached Chain Stitch; **Silk ribbon embroidery stitches:** None; **Beads and baubles:** 2 mm round bead, seed bead, sequin

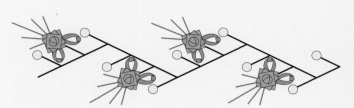

253 **Base-seam template:** Feather Stitch Base Seam 3; **Thread embroidery stitches:** Feather Stitch, Straight Stitch; **Silk ribbon embroidery stitches:** Detached Chain Stitch, Fargo Rose; **Beads and baubles:** 3 mm round bead

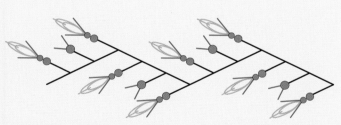

254 **Base-seam template:** Feather Stitch Base Seam 3; **Thread embroidery stitches:** Feather Stitch, Detached Chain Stitch, Straight Stitch; **Silk ribbon embroidery stitches:** None; **Beads and baubles:** Seed bead, 3 mm round bead

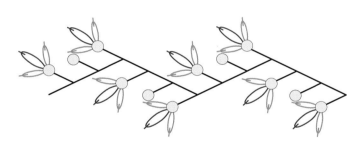

255 **Base-seam template:** Feather Stitch Base Seam 3; **Thread embroidery stitches:** Feather Stitch, Detached Chain Stitch; **Silk ribbon embroidery stitches:** None; **Beads and baubles:** 3 mm round bead

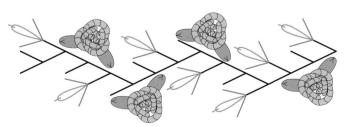

256 **Base-seam template:** Feather Stitch Base Seam 3; **Thread embroidery stitches:** Feather Stitch, Detached Chain Stitch, Bullion Stitch, Straight Stitch, French Knot; **Silk ribbon embroidery stitches:** Straight Stitch; **Beads and baubles:** None

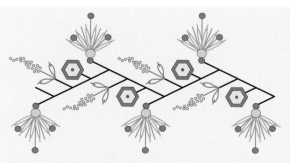

257 **Base-seam template:** Feather Stitch Base Seam 3; **Thread embroidery stitches:** Feather Stitch, Detached Chain Stitch, French Knot, Straight Stitch; **Silk ribbon embroidery stitches:** None; **Beads and baubles:** 2 mm round bead, 3 mm round bead, seed bead, sequin

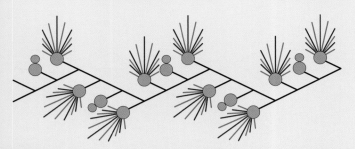

258 **Base-seam template:** Feather Stitch Base Seam 3; **Thread embroidery stitches:** Feather Stitch, Straight Stitch; **Silk ribbon embroidery stitches:** None; **Beads and baubles:** 3 mm round bead, 4 mm round bead

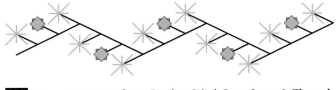

259 **Base-seam template:** Feather Stitch Base Seam 3; **Thread embroidery stitches:** Feather Stitch, Straight Stitch; **Silk ribbon embroidery stitches:** None; **Beads and baubles:** 3 mm montée

260 **Base-seam template:** Feather Stitch Base Seam 3; **Thread embroidery stitches:** Feather Stitch; **Silk ribbon embroidery stitches:** Ribbon Stitch, Straight Stitch, Detached Chain Stitch; **Beads and baubles:** 2 mm round bead

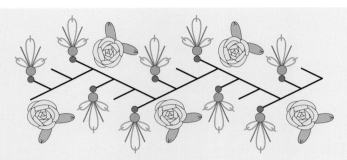

261 **Base-seam template:** Feather Stitch Base Seam 3; **Thread embroidery stitches:** Feather Stitch, Detached Chain Stitch, Straight Stitch; **Silk ribbon embroidery stitches:** Straight Stitch, Woven Rose; **Beads and baubles:** 2 mm round bead, 3 mm round bead

262 **Base-seam template:** Feather Stitch Base Seam 3; **Thread embroidery stitches:** Feather Stitch, Detached Chain Stitch, Straight Stitch; **Silk ribbon embroidery stitches:** Fargo Rose; **Beads and baubles:** None

263 **Base-seam template:** Feather Stitch Base Seam 3; **Thread embroidery stitches:** Feather Stitch, Detached Chain Stitch, Straight Stitch, French Knot; **Silk ribbon embroidery stitches:** None; **Beads and baubles:** Button

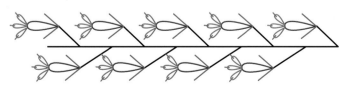

264 **Base-seam template:** Feather Stitch Base Seam 4; **Thread embroidery stitches:** Feather Stitch, Detached Chain Stitch, Straight Stitch; **Silk ribbon embroidery stitches:** None; **Beads and baubles:** None

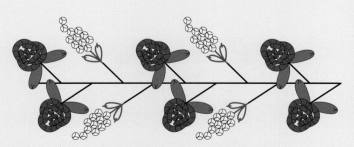

265 **Base-seam template:** Feather Stitch Base Seam 4; **Thread embroidery stitches:** Feather Stitch, Bullion Stitch, French Knot, Detached Chain Stitch, Straight Stitch; **Silk ribbon embroidery stitches:** Straight Stitch; **Beads and baubles:** None

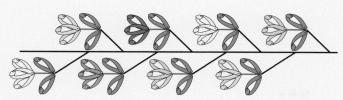

266 **Base-seam template:** Feather Stitch Base Seam 4; **Thread embroidery stitches:** Feather Stitch, Straight Stitch; **Silk ribbon embroidery stitches:** Detached Chain Stitch; **Beads and baubles:** None

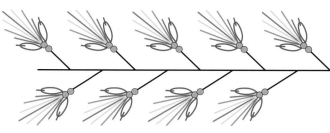

267 **Base-seam template:** Feather Stitch Base Seam 4; **Thread embroidery stitches:** Feather Stitch, Detached Chain Stitch, Straight Stitch; **Silk ribbon embroidery stitches:** None; **Beads and baubles:** 2 mm round bead

268 **Base-seam template:** Feather Stitch Base Seam 4; **Thread embroidery stitches:** Feather Stitch, Detached Chain Stitch, Straight Stitch; **Silk ribbon embroidery stitches:** None; **Beads and baubles:** Rice bead

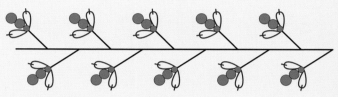

269 **Base-seam template:** Feather Stitch Base Seam 4; **Thread embroidery stitches:** Feather Stitch, Detached Chain Stitch; **Silk ribbon embroidery stitches:** None; **Beads and baubles:** 2 mm round bead, 3 mm round bead, seed bead

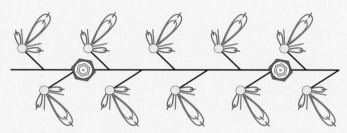

270 **Base-seam template:** Feather Stitch Base Seam 4; **Thread embroidery stitches:** Feather Stitch, Detached Chain Stitch, Straight Stitch; **Silk ribbon embroidery stitches:** None; **Beads and baubles:** 2 mm round bead, seed bead, sequin

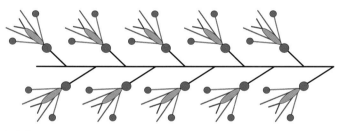

271 **Base-seam template:** Feather Stitch Base Seam 4; **Thread embroidery stitches:** Feather Stitch, Straight Stitch; **Silk ribbon embroidery stitches:** None; **Beads and baubles:** 2 mm round bead, 3 mm round bead, rice bead

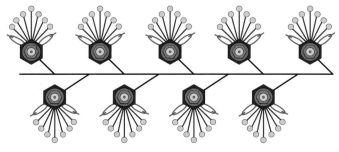

272 **Base-seam template:** Feather Stitch Base Seam 4; **Thread embroidery stitches:** Feather Stitch, Detached Chain Stitch, Straight Stitch; **Silk ribbon embroidery stitches:** None; **Beads and baubles:** Seed bead, sequin

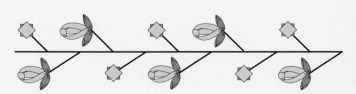

273 **Base-seam template:** Feather Stitch Base Seam 4; **Thread embroidery stitches:** Feather Stitch; **Silk ribbon embroidery stitches:** Ribbon Stitch, Straight Stitch, Detached Chain Stitch; **Beads and baubles:** 4 mm montée

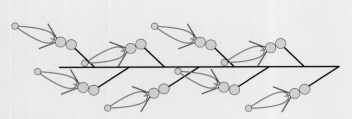

274 **Base-seam template:** Feather Stitch Base Seam 4; **Thread embroidery stitches:** Feather Stitch, Detached Chain Stitch, Straight Stitch; **Silk ribbon embroidery stitches:** None; **Beads and baubles:** 2 mm round bead, 3 mm round bead

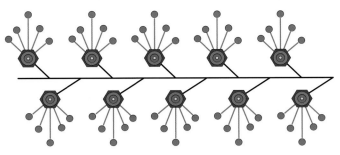

275 **Base-seam template:** Feather Stitch Base Seam 4; **Thread embroidery stitches:** Feather Stitch, Straight Stitch; **Silk ribbon embroidery stitches:** None; **Beads and baubles:** 2 mm round bead, seed bead, sequin

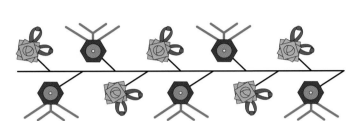

276 **Base-seam template:** Feather Stitch Base Seam 4; **Thread embroidery stitches:** Feather Stitch, Straight Stitch; **Silk ribbon embroidery stitches:** Detached Chain Stitch, Fargo Rose; **Beads and baubles:** Seed bead, sequin

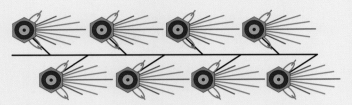

277 **Base-seam template:** Feather Stitch Base Seam 4; **Thread embroidery stitches:** Feather Stitch, Detached Chain Stitch, Straight Stitch; **Silk ribbon embroidery stitches:** None; **Beads and baubles:** Seed bead, sequin

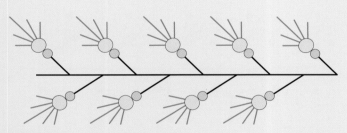

278 **Base-seam template:** Feather Stitch Base Seam 4; **Thread embroidery stitches:** Feather Stitch, Straight Stitch; **Silk ribbon embroidery stitches:** None; **Beads and baubles:** 3 mm round bead, 4 mm round bead

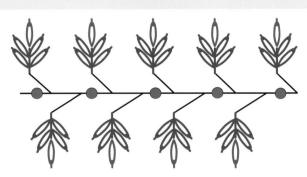

279 **Base-seam template:** Feather Stitch Base Seam 4; **Thread embroidery stitches:** Feather Stitch, Detached Chain Stitch, Straight Stitch; **Silk ribbon embroidery stitches:** None; **Beads and baubles:** 3 mm round bead

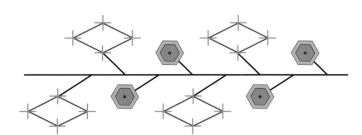

280 **Base-seam template:** Feather Stitch Base Seam 4; **Thread embroidery stitches:** Feather Stitch, Straight Stitch; **Silk ribbon embroidery stitches:** None; **Beads and baubles:** Seed bead, sequin

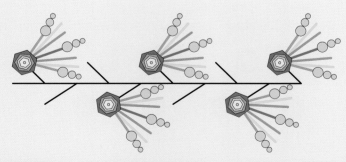

281 **Base-seam template:** Feather Stitch Base Seam 4; **Thread embroidery stitches:** Feather Stitch, Straight Stitch; **Silk ribbon embroidery stitches:** None; **Beads and baubles:** 2 mm round bead, 3 mm round bead, seed bead, sequin

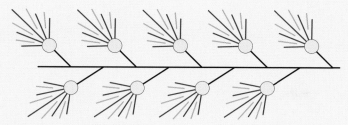

282 **Base-seam template:** Feather Stitch Base Seam 4; **Thread embroidery stitches:** Feather Stitch, Straight Stitch; **Silk ribbon embroidery stitches:** None; **Beads and baubles:** 4 mm round bead

283 **Base-seam template:** Feather Stitch Base Seam 4; **Thread embroidery stitches:** Feather Stitch, Straight Stitch; **Silk ribbon embroidery stitches:** Straight Stitch; **Beads and baubles:** 4 mm montée, size 15 rocailles

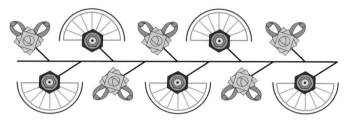

284 **Base-seam template:** Feather Stitch Base Seam 4; **Thread embroidery stitches:** Feather Stitch, Back Stitch, Straight Stitch; **Silk ribbon embroidery stitches:** Detached Chain Stitch, Fargo Rose; **Beads and baubles:** Seed bead, sequin

285 **Base-seam template:** Feather Stitch Base Seam 4; **Thread embroidery stitches:** Feather Stitch; **Silk ribbon embroidery stitches:** Detached Chain Stitch, Straight Stitch; **Beads and baubles:** Seed bead, rice bead, sequin

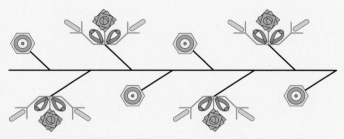

286 **Base-seam template:** Feather Stitch Base Seam 4; **Thread embroidery stitches:** Feather Stitch, Straight Stitch; **Silk ribbon embroidery stitches:** Detached Chain Stitch, Fargo Rose; **Beads and baubles:** Seed bead, bugle bead, sequin

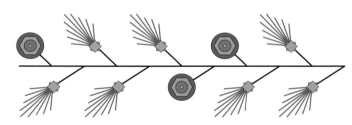

287 **Base-seam template:** Feather Stitch Base Seam 4; **Thread embroidery stitches:** Feather Stitch, Straight Stitch; **Silk ribbon embroidery stitches:** None; **Beads and baubles:** Seed bead, sequin, 3 mm montée

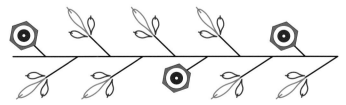

288 **Base-seam template:** Feather Stitch Base Seam 4; **Thread embroidery stitches:** Feather Stitch, Detached Chain Stitch; **Silk ribbon embroidery stitches:** None; **Beads and baubles:** Seed bead, sequin

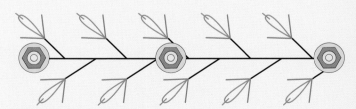

289 **Base-seam template:** Feather Stitch Base Seam 4; **Thread embroidery stitches:** Feather Stitch, Detached Chain Stitch, Straight Stitch; **Silk ribbon embroidery stitches:** None; **Beads and baubles:** 2 mm round bead, sequin

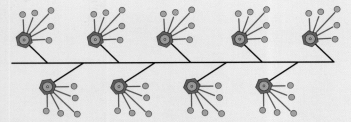

290 **Base-seam template:** Feather Stitch Base Seam 4; **Thread embroidery stitches:** Feather Stitch, Straight Stitch; **Silk ribbon embroidery stitches:** None; **Beads and baubles:** 2 mm round bead, seed bead, sequin

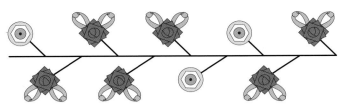

291 **Base-seam template:** Feather Stitch Base Seam 4; **Thread embroidery stitches:** Feather Stitch; **Silk ribbon embroidery stitches:** Detached Chain Stitch, Fargo Rose; **Beads and baubles:** Seed bead, sequin

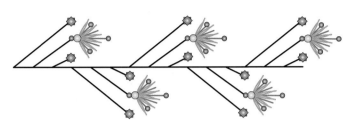

292 **Base-seam template:** Feather Stitch Base Seam 5; **Thread embroidery stitches:** Herringbone Stitch, Straight Stitch, Detached Chain Stitch; **Silk ribbon embroidery stitches:** None; **Beads and baubles:** Seed bead, 2 mm montée, 3 mm round bead

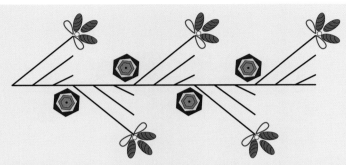

293 **Base-seam template:** Feather Stitch Base Seam 5; **Thread embroidery stitches:** Herringbone Stitch, Detached Chain Stitch, Bullion Stitch; **Silk ribbon embroidery stitches:** None; **Beads and baubles:** Seed bead

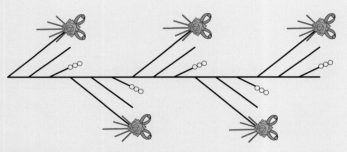

294 **Base-seam template:** Feather Stitch Base Seam 5; **Thread embroidery stitches:** Herringbone Stitch, Straight Stitch; **Silk ribbon embroidery stitches:** Detached Chain Stitch, Fargo Rose; **Beads and baubles:** Seed bead

295 **Base-seam template:** Herringbone Stitch Base Seam 1; **Thread embroidery stitches:** Herringbone Stitch, Detached Chain Stitch, Straight Stitch; **Silk ribbon embroidery stitches:** None; **Beads and baubles:** Seed bead

296 **Base-seam template:** Herringbone Stitch Base Seam 1; **Thread embroidery stitches:** Herringbone Stitch, French Knot, Straight Stitch; **Silk ribbon embroidery stitches:** Detached Chain Stitch, Straight Stitch; **Beads and baubles:** 3 mm montée

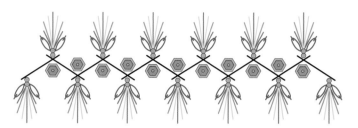

297 **Base-seam template:** Herringbone Stitch Base Seam 1; **Thread embroidery stitches:** Herringbone Stitch, Straight Stitch, Detached Chain Stitch; **Silk ribbon embroidery stitches:** None; **Beads and baubles:** Seed bead, sequin

298 **Base-seam template:** Herringbone Stitch Base Seam 1; **Thread embroidery stitches:** Herringbone Stitch, Straight Stitch, Detached Chain Stitch; **Silk ribbon embroidery stitches:** None; **Beads and baubles:** Seed bead, 2 mm round bead

299 **Base-seam template:** Herringbone Stitch Base Seam 1; **Thread embroidery stitches:** Herringbone Stitch, Straight Stitch, Detached Chain Stitch; **Silk ribbon embroidery stitches:** None; **Beads and baubles:** Seed bead

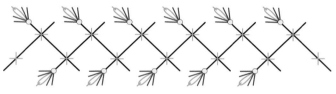

300 **Base-seam template:** Herringbone Stitch Base Seam 2; **Thread embroidery stitches:** Herringbone Stitch, Straight Stitch, Detached Chain Stitch; **Silk ribbon embroidery stitches:** None; **Beads and baubles:** Seed bead

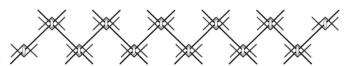

301 **Base-seam template:** Herringbone Stitch Base Seam 2; **Thread embroidery stitches:** Herringbone Stitch, Straight Stitch; **Silk ribbon embroidery stitches:** None; **Beads and baubles:** Rice bead

302 **Base-seam template:** Herringbone Stitch Base Seam 2; **Thread embroidery stitches:** Herringbone Stitch, Straight Stitch, Detached Chain Stitch; **Silk ribbon embroidery stitches:** None; **Beads and baubles:** Seed bead

303 **Base-seam template:** Herringbone Stitch Base Seam 2; **Thread embroidery stitches:** Herringbone Stitch; **Silk ribbon embroidery stitches:** Detached Chain Stitch, Fargo Rose; **Beads and baubles:** Seed bead, sequin

304 **Base-seam template:** Herringbone Stitch Base Seam 2; **Thread embroidery stitches:** Herringbone Stitch, Straight Stitch; **Silk ribbon embroidery stitches:** None; **Beads and baubles:** 3 mm round bead, 2 mm round bead, seed bead, sequin

305 **Base-seam template:** Herringbone Stitch Base Seam 2; **Thread embroidery stitches:** Herringbone Stitch, Bullion Stitch, French Knot; **Silk ribbon embroidery stitches:** Straight Stitch; **Beads and baubles:** Seed bead, rice bead, sequin

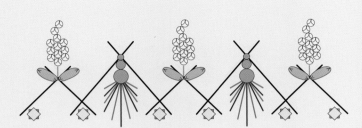

306 **Base-seam template:** Herringbone Stitch Base Seam 3; **Thread embroidery stitches:** Herringbone Stitch, Straight Stitch, French Knot; **Silk ribbon embroidery stitches:** Straight Stitch; **Beads and baubles:** 4 mm round bead, 3 mm round bead, 2 mm round bead, 3 mm montée

307 **Base-seam template:** Herringbone Stitch Base Seam 3; **Thread embroidery stitches:** Herringbone Stitch, Feather Stitch, Straight Stitch; **Silk ribbon embroidery stitches:** Straight Stitch, Ribbon Stitch, French Knot, Stem Stitch Rose; **Beads and baubles:** Seed bead, rice bead, 3 mm montée

308 **Base-seam template:** Herringbone Stitch Base Seam 3; **Thread embroidery stitches:** Herringbone Stitch, Detached Chain Stitch, Straight Stitch; **Silk ribbon embroidery stitches:** None; **Beads and baubles:** 3 mm round bead

309 **Base-seam template:** Herringbone Stitch Base Seam 3; **Thread embroidery stitches:** Herringbone Stitch, Straight Stitch, Detached Chain Stitch; **Silk ribbon embroidery stitches:** None; **Beads and baubles:** 3 mm round bead, seed bead, oval bead

310 **Base-seam template:** Herringbone Stitch Base Seam 3; **Thread embroidery stitches:** Herringbone Stitch, Straight Stitch; **Silk ribbon embroidery stitches:** Ribbon Stitch, Woven Rose; **Beads and baubles:** 3 mm montée, seed bead

311 **Base-seam template:** Herringbone Stitch Base Seam 3; **Thread embroidery stitches:** Herringbone Stitch, Straight Stitch, Detached Chain Stitch, French Knot; **Silk ribbon embroidery stitches:** Straight Stitch; **Beads and baubles:** Seed bead, sequin

312 **Base-seam template:** Herringbone Stitch Base Seam 3; **Thread embroidery stitches:** Herringbone Stitch, Straight Stitch, Detached Chain Stitch; **Silk ribbon embroidery stitches:** Fargo Rose; **Beads and baubles:** 3 mm round bead

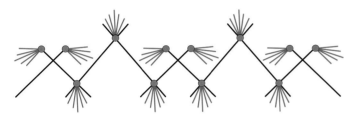

313 **Base-seam template:** Herringbone Stitch Base Seam 3; **Thread embroidery stitches:** Herringbone Stitch, Straight Stitch; **Silk ribbon embroidery stitches:** None; **Beads and baubles:** 3 mm round bead

314 **Base-seam template:** Herringbone Stitch Base Seam 3; **Thread embroidery stitches:** Herringbone Stitch, Straight Stitch, Detached Chain Stitch; **Silk ribbon embroidery stitches:** None; **Beads and baubles:** 3 mm round bead, 2 mm round bead, seed bead, sequin

315 **Base-seam template:** Herringbone Stitch Base Seam 3; **Thread embroidery stitches:** Herringbone Stitch; **Silk ribbon embroidery stitches:** Straight Stitch, Ribbon Stitch, Fargo Rose, Woven Rose; **Beads and baubles:** Seed bead, sequin

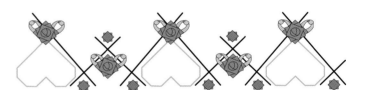

316 **Base-seam template:** Herringbone Stitch Base Seam 3; **Thread embroidery stitches:** Herringbone Stitch, Straight Stitch; **Silk ribbon embroidery stitches:** Detached Chain Stitch, Fargo Rose; **Beads and baubles:** 3 mm montée

317 **Base-seam template:** Herringbone Stitch Base Seam 3; **Thread embroidery stitches:** Herringbone Stitch, Straight Stitch, Bullion Stitch, French Knot; **Silk ribbon embroidery stitches:** Straight Stitch; **Beads and baubles:** 4 mm round bead

318 **Base-seam template:** Herringbone Stitch Base Seam 4; **Thread embroidery stitches:** Herringbone Stitch, Straight Stitch, Detached Chain Stitch; **Silk ribbon embroidery stitches:** Straight Stitch; **Beads and baubles:** Rice bead, seed bead, 3 mm montée

319 **Base-seam template:** Herringbone Stitch Base Seam 4; **Thread embroidery stitches:** Herringbone Stitch, Straight Stitch, Detached Chain Stitch; **Silk ribbon embroidery stitches:** None; **Beads and baubles:** Seed bead, sequin, 3 mm round bead, 2 mm round bead

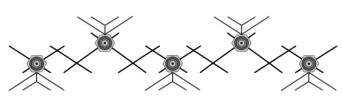

320 **Base-seam template:** Herringbone Stitch Base Seam 4; **Thread embroidery stitches:** Herringbone Stitch, Straight Stitch; **Silk ribbon embroidery stitches:** None; **Beads and baubles:** Seed bead, sequin

321 **Base-seam template:** Herringbone Stitch Base Seam 4; **Thread embroidery stitches:** Herringbone Stitch; **Silk ribbon embroidery stitches:** Straight Stitch; **Beads and baubles:** Seed bead, sequin, size 15 rocailles

322 **Base-seam template:** Herringbone Stitch Base Seam 4; **Thread embroidery stitches:** Herringbone Stitch, Straight Stitch, Detached Chain Stitch; **Silk ribbon embroidery stitches:** None; **Beads and baubles:** Seed bead, sequin, 3 mm round bead

323 **Base-seam template:** Herringbone Stitch Base Seam 4; **Thread embroidery stitches:** Herringbone Stitch, Detached Chain Stitch, Straight Stitch, French Knot, Bullion Stitch; **Silk ribbon embroidery stitches:** Detached Chain Stitch; **Beads and baubles:** Seed bead

324 **Base-seam template:** Herringbone Stitch Base Seam 4; **Thread embroidery stitches:** Herringbone Stitch, Straight Stitch, Detached Chain Stitch; **Silk ribbon embroidery stitches:** None; **Beads and baubles:** 4 mm montée, seed bead

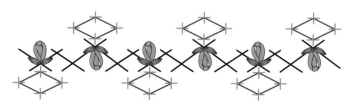

325 **Base-seam template:** Herringbone Stitch Base Seam 4; **Thread embroidery stitches:** Herringbone Stitch, Straight Stitch; **Silk ribbon embroidery stitches:** Detached Chain Stitch, Ribbon Stitch, Straight Stitch; **Beads and baubles:** None

326 **Base-seam template:** Herringbone Stitch Base Seam 4; **Thread embroidery stitches:** Herringbone Stitch, Straight Stitch, Detached Chain Stitch; **Silk ribbon embroidery stitches:** Straight Stitch, Fargo Rose; **Beads and baubles:** None

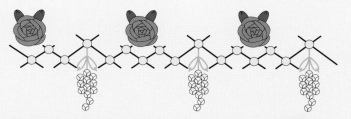

327 **Base-seam template:** Herringbone Stitch Base Seam 4; **Thread embroidery stitches:** Herringbone Stitch, Straight Stitch, French Knot, Detached Chain Stitch; **Silk ribbon embroidery stitches:** Straight Stitch, Woven Rose; **Beads and baubles:** 3 mm round bead

328 **Base-seam template:** Herringbone Stitch Base Seam 4; **Thread embroidery stitches:** Herringbone Stitch, Straight Stitch, French Knot; **Silk ribbon embroidery stitches:** Straight Stitch, Ribbon Stitch; **Beads and baubles:** 3 mm montée

329 **Base-seam template:** Herringbone Stitch Base Seam 4; **Thread embroidery stitches:** Herringbone Stitch; **Silk ribbon embroidery stitches:** Ribbon Stitch, Woven Rose; **Beads and baubles:** Seed bead

330 **Base-seam template:** Herringbone Stitch Base Seam 4; **Thread embroidery stitches:** Herringbone Stitch, Straight Stitch, Detached Chain Stitch; **Silk ribbon embroidery stitches:** None; **Beads and baubles:** Seed bead, sequin

331 **Base-seam template:** Herringbone Stitch Base Seam 4; **Thread embroidery stitches:** Herringbone Stitch, Straight Stitch, Detached Chain Stitch; **Silk ribbon embroidery stitches:** Ribbon Stitch, Straight Stitch, Detached Chain Stitch; **Beads and baubles:** 4 mm montée

332 **Base-seam template:** Herringbone Stitch Base Seam 4; **Thread embroidery stitches:** Herringbone Stitch, Detached Chain Stitch, Straight Stitch; **Silk ribbon embroidery stitches:** Straight Stitch, Fargo Rose; **Beads and baubles:** Rice bead

333 **Base-seam template:** Herringbone Stitch Base Seam 4; **Thread embroidery stitches:** Herringbone Stitch, Detached Chain Stitch, Bullion Stitch, Straight Stitch; **Silk ribbon embroidery stitches:** None; **Beads and baubles:** Seed bead

334 **Base-seam template:** Herringbone Stitch Base Seam 4; **Thread embroidery stitches:** Herringbone Stitch, Straight Stitch, Detached Chain Stitch; **Silk ribbon embroidery stitches:** Ribbon Stitch, Fargo Rose; **Beads and baubles:** Rice bead

335 **Base-seam template:** Herringbone Stitch Base Seam 4; **Thread embroidery stitches:** Herringbone Stitch; **Silk ribbon embroidery stitches:** Detached Chain Stitch, Straight Stitch, Ribbon Stitch; **Beads and baubles:** 3 mm round bead

336 **Base-seam template:** Herringbone Stitch Base Seam 4; **Thread embroidery stitches:** Herringbone Stitch, Straight Stitch, Detached Chain Stitch; **Silk ribbon embroidery stitches:** Straight Stitch; **Beads and baubles:** Seed bead, rice bead

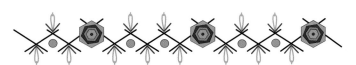

337 **Base-seam template:** Herringbone Stitch Base Seam 4; **Thread embroidery stitches:** Herringbone Stitch, Straight Stitch, Detached Chain Stitch; **Silk ribbon embroidery stitches:** None; **Beads and baubles:** Seed bead, sequin, 2 mm round bead

338 **Base-seam template:** Herringbone Stitch Base Seam 4; **Thread embroidery stitches:** Herringbone Stitch, Straight Stitch; **Silk ribbon embroidery stitches:** Detached Chain Stitch, Fargo Rose; **Beads and baubles:** 3 mm montée

339 **Base-seam template:** Herringbone Stitch Base Seam 4; **Thread embroidery stitches:** Herringbone Stitch, Straight Stitch, Detached Chain Stitch; **Silk ribbon embroidery stitches:** Detached Chain Stitch, Fargo Rose; **Beads and baubles:** 3 mm round bead, 2 mm round bead, seed bead

340 **Base-seam template:** Herringbone Stitch Base Seam 5; **Thread embroidery stitches:** Herringbone Stitch, Detached Chain Stitch; **Silk ribbon embroidery stitches:** Woven Rose, Fargo Rose; **Beads and baubles:** None

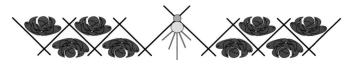

341 **Base-seam template:** Herringbone Stitch Base Seam 5; **Thread embroidery stitches:** Herringbone Stitch, Straight Stitch; **Silk ribbon embroidery stitches:** French Knot, Straight Stitch, Stem Stitch Rose; **Beads and baubles:** 4 mm round bead, 3 mm round bead

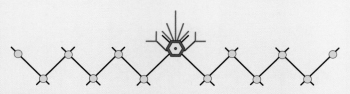

342 **Base-seam template:** Herringbone Stitch Base Seam 5; **Thread embroidery stitches:** Herringbone Stitch, Straight Stitch; **Silk ribbon embroidery stitches:** None; **Beads and baubles:** 3 mm round bead, seed bead, sequin

343 **Base-seam template:** Herringbone Stitch Base Seam 5; **Thread embroidery stitches:** Herringbone Stitch, Straight Stitch; **Silk ribbon embroidery stitches:** French Knot, Detached Chain Stitch, Wrapped Straight Stitch, Straight Stitch; **Beads and baubles:** Size 15 rocailles

344 **Base-seam template:** Herringbone Stitch Base Seam 5; **Thread embroidery stitches:** Herringbone Stitch, Straight Stitch; **Silk ribbon embroidery stitches:** Detached Chain Stitch, Fargo Rose, Straight Stitch; **Beads and baubles:** Seed bead, bugle bead

345 **Base-seam template:** Herringbone Stitch Base Seam 5; **Thread embroidery stitches:** Herringbone Stitch, Straight Stitch; **Silk ribbon embroidery stitches:** None; **Beads and baubles:** None

346 **Base-seam template:** Herringbone Stitch Base Seam 5; **Thread embroidery stitches:** Herringbone Stitch, Straight Stitch, Detached Chain Stitch; **Silk ribbon embroidery stitches:** None; **Beads and baubles:** 3 mm round bead, seed bead, sequin

347 **Base-seam template:** Herringbone Stitch Base Seam 5; **Thread embroidery stitches:** Herringbone Stitch, Detached Chain Stitch, Straight Stitch; **Silk ribbon embroidery stitches:** None; **Beads and baubles:** 3 mm round bead, seed bead

348 **Base-seam template:** Herringbone Stitch Base Seam 5; **Thread embroidery stitches:** Herringbone Stitch, Detached Chain Stitch, Straight Stitch; **Silk ribbon embroidery stitches:** None; **Beads and baubles:** Seed bead, sequin, 2 mm round bead

349 **Base-seam template:** Herringbone Stitch Base Seam 5; **Thread embroidery stitches:** Herringbone Stitch, Straight Stitch; **Silk ribbon embroidery stitches:** Detached Chain Stitch, Fargo Rose; **Beads and baubles:** Seed bead, sequin

350 **Base-seam template:** Herringbone Stitch Base Seam 5; **Thread embroidery stitches:** Herringbone Stitch, Detached Chain Stitch, Straight Stitch; **Silk ribbon embroidery stitches:** None; **Beads and baubles:** 3 mm round bead, 2 mm round bead, seed bead, sequin

351 **Base-seam template:** Herringbone Stitch Base Seam 5; **Thread embroidery stitches:** Herringbone Stitch, Straight Stitch, Detached Chain Stitch; **Silk ribbon embroidery stitches:** Detached Chain Stitch, Straight Stitch; **Beads and baubles:** Seed bead, sequin

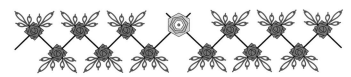

352 **Base-seam template:** Herringbone Stitch Base Seam 5; **Thread embroidery stitches:** Herringbone Stitch, Detached Chain Stitch; **Silk ribbon embroidery stitches:** Fargo Rose; **Beads and baubles:** Seed bead, sequin

353 **Base-seam template:** Herringbone Stitch Base Seam 5; **Thread embroidery stitches:** Herringbone Stitch, Straight Stitch; **Silk ribbon embroidery stitches:** Detached Chain Stitch; **Beads and baubles:** 2 mm round bead

354 **Base-seam template:** Herringbone Stitch Base Seam 5; **Thread embroidery stitches:** Herringbone Stitch, Straight Stitch; **Silk ribbon embroidery stitches:** Detached Chain Stitch, Straight Stitch; **Beads and baubles:** 3 mm montée, seed bead

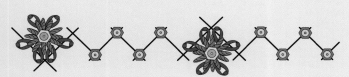

355 **Base-seam template:** Herringbone Stitch Base Seam 5; **Thread embroidery stitches:** Herringbone Stitch, Bullion Stitch; **Silk ribbon embroidery stitches:** Detached Chain Stitch; **Beads and baubles:** Seed bead, sequin

356 **Base-seam template:** Herringbone Stitch Base Seam 6; **Thread embroidery stitches:** Herringbone Stitch, Straight Stitch; **Silk ribbon embroidery stitches:** Ribbon Stitch, Woven Rose; **Beads and baubles:** 4 mm round bead

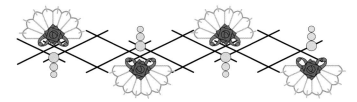

357 **Base-seam template:** Herringbone Stitch Base Seam 6; **Thread embroidery stitches:** Herringbone Stitch, Detached Chain Stitch; **Silk ribbon embroidery stitches:** Detached Chain Stitch, Fargo Rose; **Beads and baubles:** 3 mm round bead, 2 mm round bead, seed bead

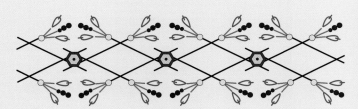

358 **Base-seam template:** Herringbone Stitch Base Seam 6; **Thread embroidery stitches:** Herringbone Stitch, Straight Stitch, Detached Chain Stitch; **Silk ribbon embroidery stitches:** None; **Beads and baubles:** Seed bead, sequin, 2 mm round bead, 3 mm round bead

359 **Base-seam template:** Herringbone Stitch Base Seam 6;
Thread embroidery stitches: Herringbone Stitch, Straight
Stitch; **Silk ribbon embroidery stitches:** Straight Stitch, Woven
Rose; **Beads and baubles:** 3 mm round bead, seed bead, sequin

360 **Base-seam template:** Herringbone Stitch Base Seam 6;
Thread embroidery stitches: Herringbone Stitch, Straight
Stitch, Detached Chain Stitch, French Knot; **Silk ribbon
embroidery stitches:** None; **Beads and baubles:** 2 mm montée

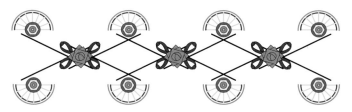

361 **Base-seam template:** Herringbone Stitch Base Seam 6;
Thread embroidery stitches: Herringbone Stitch, Straight
Stitch, Back Stitch; **Silk ribbon embroidery stitches:** Detached
Chain Stitch, Fargo Rose; **Beads and baubles:** Seed bead, sequin

362 **Base-seam template:** Herringbone Stitch Base Seam 6;
Thread embroidery stitches: Herringbone Stitch, French Knot;
Silk ribbon embroidery stitches: Detached Chain Stitch, French
Knot, Straight Stitch; **Beads and baubles:** None

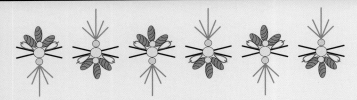

363 **Base-seam template:** Straight Stitch Base Seam 1; **Thread embroidery stitches:** Straight Stitch, Detached Chain Stitch, Bullion Stitch; **Silk ribbon embroidery stitches:** None; **Beads and baubles:** Seed bead, 2 mm round bead, 3 mm round bead

364 **Base-seam template:** Straight Stitch Base Seam 1; **Thread embroidery stitches:** Straight Stitch, Back Stitch; **Silk ribbon embroidery stitches:** None; **Beads and baubles:** Seed bead, sequin

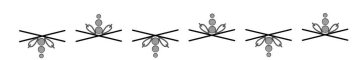

365 **Base-seam template:** Straight Stitch Base Seam 1; **Thread embroidery stitches:** Straight Stitch, Detached Chain Stitch; **Silk ribbon embroidery stitches:** None; **Beads and baubles:** Seed bead, 2 mm round bead, 3 mm round bead

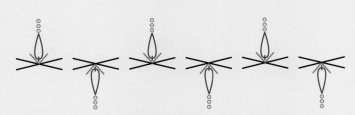

366 **Base-seam template:** Straight Stitch Base Seam 1; **Thread embroidery stitches:** Straight Stitch, Detached Chain Stitch; **Silk ribbon embroidery stitches:** None; **Beads and baubles:** Seed bead

367 **Base-seam template:** Straight Stitch Base Seam 1; **Thread embroidery stitches:** Straight Stitch; **Silk ribbon embroidery stitches:** Detached Chain Stitch; **Beads and baubles:** Seed bead, sequin, 2 mm round bead, 3 mm round bead, 4 mm montée

368 **Base-seam template:** Straight Stitch Base Seam 1; **Thread embroidery stitches:** Straight Stitch, Detached Chain Stitch (Note that the Detached Chain Stitches used here have a wider base; A and B are set farther apart than usual.); **Silk ribbon embroidery stitches:** Detached Chain Stitch, Fargo Rose; **Beads and baubles:** Seed bead, sequin

369 **Base-seam template:** Straight Stitch Base Seam 1; **Thread embroidery stitches:** Straight Stitch; **Silk ribbon embroidery stitches:** None; **Beads and baubles:** Seed bead, 3 mm round bead, 2 mm round bead

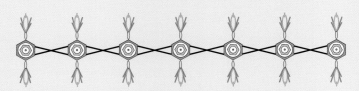

370 **Base-seam template:** Straight Stitch Base Seam 1; **Thread embroidery stitches:** Straight Stitch, Detached Chain Stitch; **Silk ribbon embroidery stitches:** None; **Beads and baubles:** Seed bead, sequin, rice bead

371 **Base-seam template:** Straight Stitch Base Seam 1; **Thread embroidery stitches:** Straight Stitch; **Silk ribbon embroidery stitches:** Straight Stitch, Detached Chain Stitch; **Beads and baubles:** Seed bead, sequin, 2 mm round bead

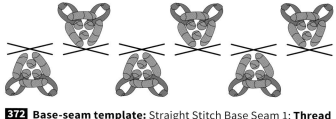

372 **Base-seam template:** Straight Stitch Base Seam 1; **Thread embroidery stitches:** Straight Stitch; **Silk ribbon embroidery stitches:** Detached Chain Stitch, French Knot, Wrapped Straight Stitch; **Beads and baubles:** None

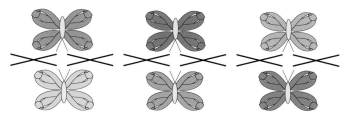

373 **Base-seam template:** Straight Stitch Base Seam 1; **Thread embroidery stitches:** Straight Stitch; **Silk ribbon embroidery stitches:** Detached Chain Stitch, Straight Stitch; **Beads and baubles:** Rice bead

374 **Base-seam template:** Straight Stitch Base Seam 1; **Thread embroidery stitches:** Straight Stitch; **Silk ribbon embroidery stitches:** Detached Chain Stitch; **Beads and baubles:** Flower cap bead, seed bead

375 **Base-seam template:** Straight Stitch Base Seam 1; **Thread embroidery stitches:** Straight Stitch, French Knot; **Silk ribbon embroidery stitches:** Straight Stitch; **Beads and baubles:** 4 mm round bead

376 **Base-seam template:** Straight Stitch Base Seam 1; **Thread embroidery stitches:** Straight Stitch; **Silk ribbon embroidery stitches:** Detached Chain Stitch, Fargo Rose; **Beads and baubles:** 4 mm montée

377 **Base-seam template:** Straight Stitch Base Seam 1; **Thread embroidery stitches:** Straight Stitch; **Silk ribbon embroidery stitches:** Detached Chain Stitch, Fargo Rose; **Beads and baubles:** None

378 **Base-seam template:** Straight Stitch Base Seam 1; **Thread embroidery stitches:** Straight Stitch, Bullion Stitch; **Silk ribbon embroidery stitches:** Detached Chain Stitch; **Beads and baubles:** 4 mm montée, 2 mm round bead

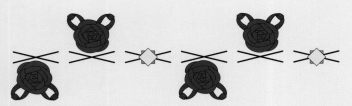

379 **Base-seam template:** Straight Stitch Base Seam 1; **Thread embroidery stitches:** Straight Stitch; **Silk ribbon embroidery stitches:** Detached Chain Stitch, Woven Rose; **Beads and baubles:** 4 mm montée

380 **Base-seam template:** Straight Stitch Base Seam 1; **Thread embroidery stitches:** Straight Stitch, Detached Chain Stitch, Bullion Stitch; **Silk ribbon embroidery stitches:** None; **Beads and baubles:** Seed bead

381 **Base-seam template:** Straight Stitch Base Seam 1; **Thread embroidery stitches:** Straight Stitch; **Silk ribbon embroidery stitches:** Detached Chain Stitch, Straight Stitch, Ribbon Stitch; **Beads and baubles:** Seed bead, sequin

382 **Base-seam template:** Straight Stitch Base Seam 2; **Thread embroidery stitches:** Straight Stitch, Detached Chain Stitch; **Silk ribbon embroidery stitches:** None; **Beads and baubles:** Seed bead

383 **Base-seam template:** Straight Stitch Base Seam 2; **Thread embroidery stitches:** Straight Stitch, Detached Chain Stitch; **Silk ribbon embroidery stitches:** Detached Chain Stitch, Fargo Rose; **Beads and baubles:** Seed bead

384 **Base-seam template:** Straight Stitch Base Seam 2; **Thread embroidery stitches:** Straight Stitch; **Silk ribbon embroidery stitches:** Detached Chain Stitch, Fargo Rose; **Beads and baubles:** None

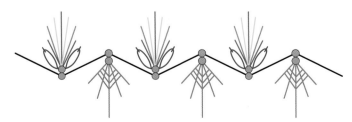

385 **Base-seam template:** Straight Stitch Base Seam 2; **Thread embroidery stitches:** Straight Stitch, Detached Chain Stitch; **Silk ribbon embroidery stitches:** None; **Beads and baubles:** Seed bead

386 **Base-seam template:** Straight Stitch Base Seam 2; **Thread embroidery stitches:** Straight Stitch; **Silk ribbon embroidery stitches:** Straight Stitch, Detached Chain Stitch; **Beads and baubles:** Seed bead, sequin

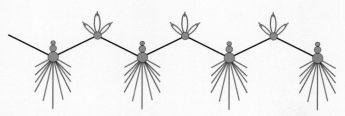

387 **Base-seam template:** Straight Stitch Base Seam 2; **Thread embroidery stitches:** Straight Stitch, Detached Chain Stitch; **Silk ribbon embroidery stitches:** None; **Beads and baubles:** 3 mm round bead, 2 mm round bead, seed bead

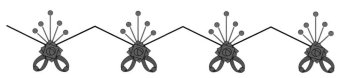

388 **Base-seam template:** Straight Stitch Base Seam 2; **Thread embroidery stitches:** Straight Stitch; **Silk ribbon embroidery stitches:** Detached Chain Stitch, Fargo Rose; **Beads and baubles:** Seed bead

389 **Base-seam template:** Straight Stitch Base Seam 2; **Thread embroidery stitches:** Straight Stitch, Detached Chain Stitch; **Silk ribbon embroidery stitches:** None; **Beads and baubles:** Seed bead, sequin

390 **Base-seam template:** Straight Stitch Base Seam 2; **Thread embroidery stitches:** Straight Stitch, Detached Chain Stitch; **Silk ribbon embroidery stitches:** Detached Chain Stitch, Fargo Rose; **Beads and baubles:** None

391 **Base-seam template:** Straight Stitch Base Seam 2; **Thread embroidery stitches:** Straight Stitch, Detached Chain Stitch; **Silk ribbon embroidery stitches:** Detached Chain Stitch, Fargo Rose; **Beads and baubles:** None

392 **Base-seam template:** Straight Stitch Base Seam 2; **Thread embroidery stitches:** Straight Stitch, Detached Chain Stitch; **Silk ribbon embroidery stitches:** None; **Beads and baubles:** Seed bead, sequin, 2 mm round bead

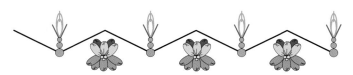

393 **Base-seam template:** Straight Stitch Base Seam 2; **Thread embroidery stitches:** Straight Stitch, Detached Chain Stitch; **Silk ribbon embroidery stitches:** Straight Stitch; **Beads and baubles:** 3 mm round bead, 2 mm round bead, seed bead, size 15 rocailles

394 **Base-seam template:** Straight Stitch Base Seam 2; **Thread embroidery stitches:** Straight Stitch, Detached Chain Stitch, Bullion Stitch; **Silk ribbon embroidery stitches:** Detached Chain Stitch; **Beads and baubles:** Seed bead, sequin

395 **Base-seam template:** Straight Stitch Base Seam 2; **Thread embroidery stitches:** Straight Stitch, Detached Chain Stitch; **Silk ribbon embroidery stitches:** None; **Beads and baubles:** 2 mm round bead, button

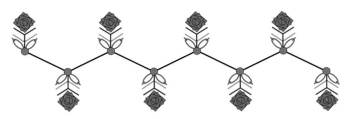

396 **Base-seam template:** Straight Stitch Base Seam 2; **Thread embroidery stitches:** Straight Stitch, Detached Chain Stitch; **Silk ribbon embroidery stitches:** Fargo Rose; **Beads and baubles:** 3 mm round bead

397 **Base-seam template:** Straight Stitch Base Seam 2; **Thread embroidery stitches:** Straight Stitch; **Silk ribbon embroidery stitches:** Straight Stitch; **Beads and baubles:** 3 mm round bead, 2 mm round bead, size 15 rocailles

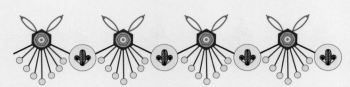

398 **Base-seam template:** Straight Stitch Base Seam 2; **Thread embroidery stitches:** Straight Stitch, Detached Chain Stitch, Bullion Stitch; **Silk ribbon embroidery stitches:** None; **Beads and baubles:** Seed bead, sequin, 3 mm round bead, button

399 **Base-seam template:** Straight Stitch Base Seam 2; **Thread embroidery stitches:** Straight Stitch, Bullion Stitch; **Silk ribbon embroidery stitches:** Ribbon Stitch; **Beads and baubles:** 3 mm round bead, seed bead, sequin

400 **Base-seam template:** Straight Stitch Base Seam 2; **Thread embroidery stitches:** Straight Stitch; **Silk ribbon embroidery stitches:** Detached Chain Stitch; **Beads and baubles:** Seed bead, sequin, button

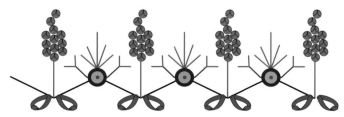

401 **Base-seam template:** Straight Stitch Base Seam 2; **Thread embroidery stitches:** Straight Stitch, French Knot; **Silk ribbon embroidery stitches:** Detached Chain Stitch; **Beads and baubles:** Seed bead, sequin

402 **Base-seam template:** Straight Stitch Base Seam 2; **Thread embroidery stitches:** Straight Stitch, Bullion Stitch, French Knot, Detached Chain Stitch; **Silk ribbon embroidery stitches:** Detached Chain Stitch; **Beads and baubles:** 3 mm round bead, seed bead

403 Base-seam template: Straight Stitch Base Seam 2; **Thread embroidery stitches:** Straight Stitch, Detached Chain Stitch, French Knot, Bullion Stitch; **Silk ribbon embroidery stitches:** Detached Chain Stitch; **Beads and baubles:** Seed bead, sequin, heart button

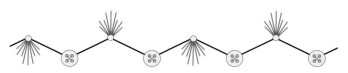

404 Base-seam template: Straight Stitch Base Seam 2; **Thread embroidery stitches:** Straight Stitch; **Silk ribbon embroidery stitches:** None; **Beads and baubles:** Seed bead, button

405 Base-seam template: Straight Stitch Base Seam 2; **Thread embroidery stitches:** Straight Stitch, French Knot; **Silk ribbon embroidery stitches:** Detached Chain Stitch; **Beads and baubles:** Seed bead, sequin

406 Base-seam template: Straight Stitch Base Seam 2; **Thread embroidery stitches:** Straight Stitch, Detached Chain Stitch; **Silk ribbon embroidery stitches:** None; **Beads and baubles:** 2 mm round bead, seed bead

407 Base-seam template: Straight Stitch Base Seam 2; **Thread embroidery stitches:** Straight Stitch; **Silk ribbon embroidery stitches:** None; **Beads and baubles:** Seed bead

408 Base-seam template: Straight Stitch Base Seam 2; **Thread embroidery stitches:** Straight Stitch, Detached Chain Stitch, Bullion Stitch; **Silk ribbon embroidery stitches:** None; **Beads and baubles:** Seed bead, 2 mm round bead

409 Base-seam template: Straight Stitch Base Seam 2; **Thread embroidery stitches:** Straight Stitch, Detached Chain Stitch, Bullion Stitch; **Silk ribbon embroidery stitches:** None; **Beads and baubles:** Seed bead

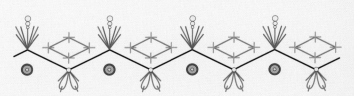

410 Base-seam template: Straight Stitch Base Seam 2; **Thread embroidery stitches:** Straight Stitch, Detached Chain Stitch; **Silk ribbon embroidery stitches:** None; **Beads and baubles:** 3 mm round bead, 2 mm round bead, seed bead, sequin

411 **Base-seam template:** Straight Stitch Base Seam 3; **Thread embroidery stitches:** Straight Stitch, Detached Chain Stitch; **Silk ribbon embroidery stitches:** None; **Beads and baubles:** 3 mm round bead, 2 mm round bead, seed bead, sequin

412 **Base-seam template:** Straight Stitch Base Seam 3; **Thread embroidery stitches:** Straight Stitch, Detached Chain Stitch, Bullion Stitch; **Silk ribbon embroidery stitches:** None; **Beads and baubles:** Seed bead, sequin, 2 mm round bead, 3 mm round bead

413 **Base-seam template:** Straight Stitch Base Seam 3; **Thread embroidery stitches:** Straight Stitch, Detached Chain Stitch, French Knot; **Silk ribbon embroidery stitches:** None; **Beads and baubles:** Seed bead, sequin

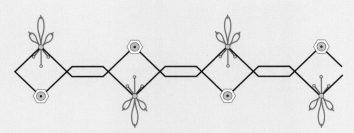

414 **Base-seam template:** Straight Stitch Base Seam 3; **Thread embroidery stitches:** Straight Stitch, Detached Chain Stitch; **Silk ribbon embroidery stitches:** None; **Beads and baubles:** Seed bead, sequin

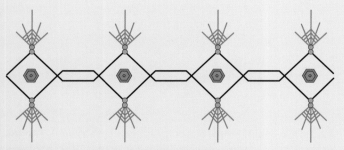

415 **Base-seam template:** Straight Stitch Base Seam 3; **Thread embroidery stitches:** Straight Stitch; **Silk ribbon embroidery stitches:** None; **Beads and baubles:** Seed bead, sequin, 3 mm round bead

416 **Base-seam template:** Straight Stitch Base Seam 3; **Thread embroidery stitches:** Straight Stitch; **Silk ribbon embroidery stitches:** Detached Chain Stitch, French Knot, Wrapped Straight Stitch; **Beads and baubles:** 2 mm round bead, 3 mm round bead, seed bead, sequin

417 **Base-seam template:** Straight Stitch Base Seam 3; **Thread embroidery stitches:** Straight Stitch, Detached Chain Stitch, Bullion Stitch; **Silk ribbon embroidery stitches:** None; **Beads and baubles:** Seed bead, 2 mm round bead

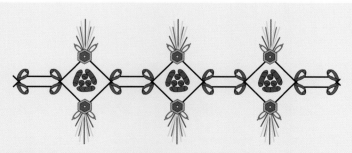

418 **Base-seam template:** Straight Stitch Base Seam 3; **Thread embroidery stitches:** Straight Stitch, Detached Chain Stitch; **Silk ribbon embroidery stitches:** Detached Chain Stitch, French Knot, Wrapped Straight Stitch; **Beads and baubles:** Seed bead, sequin

419 **Base-seam template:** Straight Stitch Base Seam 3; **Thread embroidery stitches:** Straight Stitch; **Silk ribbon embroidery stitches:** Straight Stitch, French Knot, Detached Chain Stitch; **Beads and baubles:** Seed bead, sequin

420 **Base-seam template:** Straight Stitch Base Seam 3; **Thread embroidery stitches:** Straight Stitch; **Silk ribbon embroidery stitches:** Straight Stitch; **Beads and baubles:** 2 mm round bead, 3 mm round bead, size 15 rocailles

421 **Base-seam template:** Straight Stitch Base Seam 3; **Thread embroidery stitches:** Straight Stitch, Detached Chain Stitch, Bullion Stitch; **Silk ribbon embroidery stitches:** None; **Beads and baubles:** Seed bead, 2 mm round bead

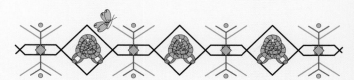

422 **Base-seam template:** Straight Stitch Base Seam 3; **Thread embroidery stitches:** Straight Stitch, Bullion Stitch, French Knot; **Silk ribbon embroidery stitches:** Detached Chain Stitch, Straight Stitch; **Beads and baubles:** Seed bead, 3 mm montée, rice bead

423 **Base-seam template:** Straight Stitch Base Seam 3; **Thread embroidery stitches:** Straight Stitch; **Silk ribbon embroidery stitches:** French Knot, Stem Stitch Rose, Detached Chain Stitch; **Beads and baubles:** 3 mm montée

424 **Base-seam template:** Straight Stitch Base Seam 3; **Thread embroidery stitches:** Straight Stitch, Detached Chain Stitch; **Silk ribbon embroidery stitches:** Detached Chain Stitch, Woven Rose; **Beads and baubles:** 3 mm round bead, 2 mm round bead, seed bead

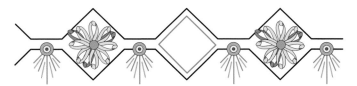

425 **Base-seam template:** Straight Stitch Base Seam 4; **Thread embroidery stitches:** Straight Stitch; **Silk ribbon embroidery stitches:** Detached Chain Stitch; **Beads and baubles:** Seed bead, sequin, 3 mm round bead

426 **Base-seam template:** Straight Stitch Base Seam 4; **Thread embroidery stitches:** Straight Stitch, Bullion Stitch; **Silk ribbon embroidery stitches:** Detached Chain Stitch; **Beads and baubles:** Seed bead, rice bead

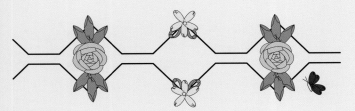

427 **Base-seam template:** Straight Stitch Base Seam 4; **Thread embroidery stitches:** Straight Stitch; **Silk ribbon embroidery stitches:** Detached Chain Stitch, Straight Stitch, Ribbon Stitch, Woven Rose; **Beads and baubles:** Seed bead, rice bead

428 **Base-seam template:** Straight Stitch Base Seam 4; **Thread embroidery stitches:** Straight Stitch; **Silk ribbon embroidery stitches:** Detached Chain Stitch, Fargo Rose; **Beads and baubles:** Seed bead, 2 mm round bead, 3 mm round bead

429 **Base-seam template:** Straight Stitch Base Seam 4; **Thread embroidery stitches:** Straight Stitch, Detached Chain Stitch, French Knot; **Silk ribbon embroidery stitches:** None; **Beads and baubles:** Seed bead, 2 mm round bead

430 **Base-seam template:** Straight Stitch Base Seam 4; **Thread embroidery stitches:** Straight Stitch, French Knot; **Silk ribbon embroidery stitches:** Detached Chain Stitch; **Beads and baubles:** Seed bead, sequin

431 **Base-seam template:** Straight Stitch Base Seam 4; **Thread embroidery stitches:** Straight Stitch, Bullion Stitch, French Knot; **Silk ribbon embroidery stitches:** Straight Stitch; **Beads and baubles:** Seed bead, sequin, 2 mm round bead, 3 mm round bead

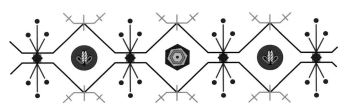

432 **Base-seam template:** Straight Stitch Base Seam 4; **Thread embroidery stitches:** Straight Stitch, Detached Chain Stitch, Bullion Stitch; **Silk ribbon embroidery stitches:** None; **Beads and baubles:** Seed bead, sequin, 3 mm montée, button

433 **Base-seam template:** Straight Stitch Base Seam 4; **Thread embroidery stitches:** Straight Stitch, Detached Chain Stitch; **Silk ribbon embroidery stitches:** Straight Stitch; **Beads and baubles:** Seed bead, sequin, size 15 rocailles

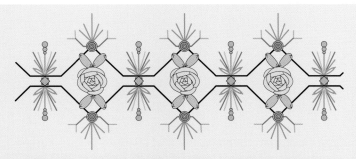

434 **Base-seam template:** Straight Stitch Base Seam 4; **Thread embroidery stitches:** Straight Stitch, Detached Chain Stitch; **Silk ribbon embroidery stitches:** Straight Stitch, Woven Rose; **Beads and baubles:** Seed bead, 2 mm round bead, 3 mm round bead, 3 mm montée, sequin

435 **Base-seam template:** Straight Stitch Base Seam 4; **Thread embroidery stitches:** Straight Stitch; **Silk ribbon embroidery stitches:** Straight Stitch, Detached Chain Stitch; **Beads and baubles:** Rice bead, 3 mm montée

436 **Base-seam template:** Straight Stitch Base Seam 4; **Thread embroidery stitches:** Straight Stitch, Detached Chain Stitch; **Silk ribbon embroidery stitches:** None; **Beads and baubles:** Seed bead, 2 mm round bead, 3 mm round bead

437 **Base-seam template:** Straight Stitch Base Seam 4; **Thread embroidery stitches:** Straight Stitch, French Knot, Detached Chain Stitch; **Silk ribbon embroidery stitches:** Straight Stitch; **Beads and baubles:** Seed bead, sequin, 3 mm round bead

438 **Base-seam template:** Straight Stitch Base Seam 4; **Thread embroidery stitches:** Straight Stitch, French Knot, Detached Chain Stitch; **Silk ribbon embroidery stitches:** Straight Stitch; **Beads and baubles:** Seed bead, 2 mm round bead, 3 mm round bead

439 **Base-seam template:** Straight Stitch Base Seam 5; **Thread embroidery stitches:** Straight Stitch, Back Stitch; **Silk ribbon embroidery stitches:** Ribbon Stitch, Fargo Rose; **Beads and baubles:** Seed bead, sequin, 3 mm montée

440 **Base-seam template:** Straight Stitch Base Seam 5; **Thread embroidery stitches:** Straight Stitch, French Knot, Bullion Stitch; **Silk ribbon embroidery stitches:** Detached Chain Stitch; **Beads and baubles:** Seed bead, button

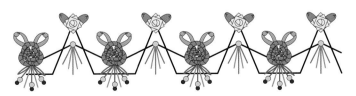

441 **Base-seam template:** Straight Stitch Base Seam 5; **Thread embroidery stitches:** Straight Stitch, Detached Chain Stitch, Bullion Stitch, French Knot; **Silk ribbon embroidery stitches:** Detached Chain Stitch, Straight Stitch, Fargo Rose; **Beads and baubles:** Seed bead

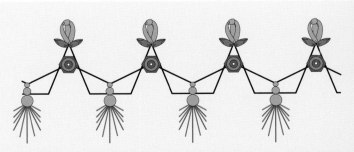

442 **Base-seam template:** Straight Stitch Base Seam 5; **Thread embroidery stitches:** Straight Stitch; **Silk ribbon embroidery stitches:** Straight Stitch, Ribbon Stitch, Detached Chain Stitch; **Beads and baubles:** 4 mm round bead, 3 mm round bead, 2 mm round bead, seed bead, sequin

443 **Base-seam template:** Straight Stitch Base Seam 5; **Thread embroidery stitches:** Straight Stitch, Detached Chain Stitch; **Silk ribbon embroidery stitches:** Straight Stitch, Detached Chain Stitch; **Beads and baubles:** 3 mm round bead

444 **Base-seam template:** Straight Stitch Base Seam 5; **Thread embroidery stitches:** Straight Stitch; **Silk ribbon embroidery stitches:** Detached Chain; **Beads and baubles:** 2 mm round bead, seed bead

445 **Base-seam template:** Straight Stitch Base Seam 5; **Thread embroidery stitches:** Straight Stitch; **Silk ribbon embroidery stitches:** Detached Chain Stitch, Straight Stitch, Ribbon Stitch; **Beads and baubles:** Seed bead, sequin, 2 mm round bead, 3 mm montée, size 15 rocailles

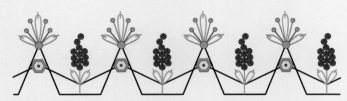

446 **Base-seam template:** Straight Stitch Base Seam 5; **Thread embroidery stitches:** Straight Stitch, Detached Chain Stitch, French Knot; **Silk ribbon embroidery stitches:** None; **Beads and baubles:** Seed bead, sequin, 3 mm round bead

447 **Base-seam template:** Straight Stitch Base Seam 5; **Thread embroidery stitches:** Straight Stitch, Detached Chain Stitch; **Silk ribbon embroidery stitches:** Straight Stitch, French Knot, Detached Chain Stitch; **Beads and baubles:** Seed bead, sequin, 2 mm round bead, 3 mm round bead, rice bead

448 **Base-seam template:** Straight Stitch Base Seam 5; **Thread embroidery stitches:** Straight Stitch, Detached Chain Stitch (Note that the Detached Chain Stitches used here have a wider base; A and B are set farther apart than usual.), Bullion Stitch, French Knot; **Silk ribbon embroidery stitches:** Detached Chain Stitch, Straight Stitch; **Beads and baubles:** Seed bead, 2 mm round bead, 3 mm montée

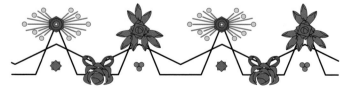

449 **Base-seam template:** Straight Stitch Base Seam 5; **Thread embroidery stitches:** Straight Stitch; **Silk ribbon embroidery stitches:** Detached Chain Stitch, Ribbon Stitch, French Knot, Fargo Rose, Stem Stitch Rose; **Beads and baubles:** Seed bead, sequin, 3 mm montée

450 **Base-seam template:** Straight Stitch Base Seam 5; **Thread embroidery stitches:** Straight Stitch, Detached Chain Stitch, Bullion Stitch; **Silk ribbon embroidery stitches:** Detached Chain Stitch, Fargo Rose; **Beads and baubles:** Seed bead, 3 mm montée

451 **Base-seam template:** Straight Stitch Base Seam 6; **Thread embroidery stitches:** Straight Stitch, Detached Chain Stitch; **Silk ribbon embroidery stitches:** Detached Chain Stitch, Fargo Rose; **Beads and baubles:** Seed bead

452 **Base-seam template:** Straight Stitch Base Seam 6; **Thread embroidery stitches:** Straight Stitch, Detached Chain Stitch, French Knot; **Silk ribbon embroidery stitches:** Detached Chain Stitch; **Beads and baubles:** Seed bead, sequin

453 **Base-seam template:** Straight Stitch Base Seam 6; **Thread embroidery stitches:** Straight Stitch, French Knot; **Silk ribbon embroidery stitches:** Straight Stitch, Detached Chain Stitch; **Beads and baubles:** Seed bead, sequin, 3 mm montée

454 **Base-seam template:** Straight Stitch Base Seam 6; **Thread embroidery stitches:** Straight Stitch, Detached Chain Stitch, French Knot; **Silk ribbon embroidery stitches:** None; **Beads and baubles:** Seed bead, sequin, 3 mm montée

455 **Base-seam template:** Straight Stitch Base Seam 6; **Thread embroidery stitches:** Straight Stitch, Detached Chain Stitch; **Silk ribbon embroidery stitches:** Ribbon Stitch, Woven Rose; **Beads and baubles:** Seed bead, sequin, 2 mm round bead, 3 mm round bead

456 **Base-seam template:** Straight Stitch Base Seam 6; **Thread embroidery stitches:** Straight Stitch, Detached Chain Stitch; **Silk ribbon embroidery stitches:** None; **Beads and baubles:** Seed bead, 3 mm montée

457 **Base-seam template:** Straight Stitch Base Seam 6; **Thread embroidery stitches:** Straight Stitch; **Silk ribbon embroidery stitches:** Detached Chain Stitch, French Knot, Stem Stitch Rose; **Beads and baubles:** 3 mm round bead

458 **Base-seam template:** Straight Stitch Base Seam 6; **Thread embroidery stitches:** Straight Stitch, Detached Chain Stitch; **Silk ribbon embroidery stitches:** None; **Beads and baubles:** Seed bead, 2 mm round bead, 3 mm round bead

459 **Base-seam template:** Straight Stitch Base Seam 6; **Thread embroidery stitches:** Straight Stitch, Detached Chain Stitch, Bullion Stitch; **Silk ribbon embroidery stitches:** Detached Chain Stitch; **Beads and baubles:** Seed bead, 3 mm round bead

460 **Base-seam template:** Straight Stitch Base Seam 6; **Thread embroidery stitches:** Straight Stitch, Detached Chain Stitch, French Knot; **Silk ribbon embroidery stitches:** Detached Chain Stitch; **Beads and baubles:** Seed bead

461 **Base-seam template:** Straight Stitch Base Seam 6; **Thread embroidery stitches:** Straight Stitch, Detached Chain Stitch, Bullion Stitch; **Silk ribbon embroidery stitches:** None; **Beads and baubles:** Seed bead

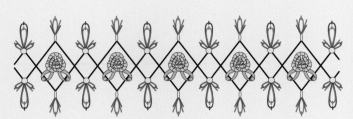

462 **Base-seam template:** Straight Stitch Base Seam 6; **Thread embroidery stitches:** Straight Stitch, Detached Chain Stitch, Bullion Stitch, French Knot; **Silk ribbon embroidery stitches:** Detached Chain Stitch; **Beads and baubles:** Seed bead, rice bead

463 **Base-seam template:** Straight Stitch Base Seam 6; **Thread embroidery stitches:** Straight Stitch; **Silk ribbon embroidery stitches:** Straight Stitch, Detached Chain Stitch; **Beads and baubles:** Seed bead, sequin, 2 mm round bead, 3 mm round bead

464 **Base-seam template:** Straight Stitch Base Seam 6; **Thread embroidery stitches:** Straight Stitch; **Silk ribbon embroidery stitches:** Detached Chain Stitch, Fargo Rose; **Beads and baubles:** Seed bead, sequin, bugle bead

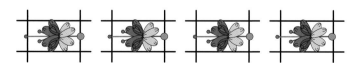

465 **Base-seam template:** Straight Stitch Base Seam 7; **Thread embroidery stitches:** Straight Stitch; **Silk ribbon embroidery stitches:** Straight Stitch, Detached Chain Stitch; **Beads and baubles:** Seed bead, 3 mm round bead

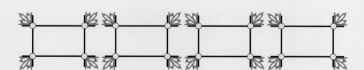

466 **Base-seam template:** Straight Stitch Base Seam 7; **Thread embroidery stitches:** Straight Stitch, Detached Chain Stitch; **Silk ribbon embroidery stitches:** None; **Beads and baubles:** Seed bead

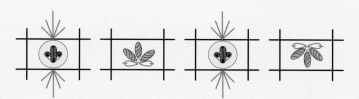

467 **Base-seam template:** Straight Stitch Base Seam 7; **Thread embroidery stitches:** Straight Stitch, Detached Chain Stitch, Bullion Stitch; **Silk ribbon embroidery stitches:** None; **Beads and baubles:** 4-hole button

468 **Base-seam template:** Straight Stitch Base Seam 7; **Thread embroidery stitches:** Straight Stitch, Detached Chain Stitch, French Knot; **Silk ribbon embroidery stitches:** None; **Beads and baubles:** Seed bead, sequin, 2 mm round bead

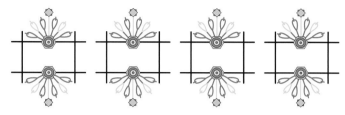

469 **Base-seam template:** Straight Stitch Base Seam 7; **Thread embroidery stitches:** Straight Stitch, Detached Chain Stitch; **Silk ribbon embroidery stitches:** None; **Beads and baubles:** Seed bead, sequin, 3 mm montée

470 **Base-seam template:** Straight Stitch Base Seam 7; **Thread embroidery stitches:** Straight Stitch, Detached Chain Stitch; **Silk ribbon embroidery stitches:** Ribbon Stitch, Woven Rose; **Beads and baubles:** Seed bead, 3 mm round bead

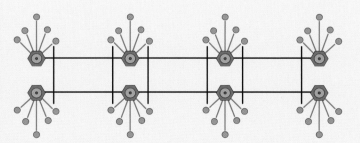

471 **Base-seam template:** Straight Stitch Base Seam 7; **Thread embroidery stitches:** Straight Stitch; **Silk ribbon embroidery stitches:** None; **Beads and baubles:** Seed bead, sequin, 2 mm round bead

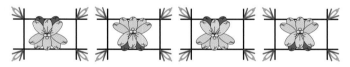

472 **Base-seam template:** Straight Stitch Base Seam 7; **Thread embroidery stitches:** Straight Stitch, Detached Chain Stitch; **Silk ribbon embroidery stitches:** Straight Stitch; **Beads and baubles:** Size 15 rocailles

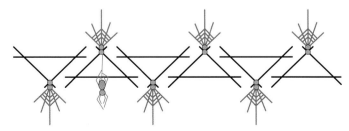

473 **Base-seam template:** Straight Stitch Base Seam 8; **Thread embroidery stitches:** Straight Stitch; **Silk ribbon embroidery stitches:** None; **Beads and baubles:** Seed bead, oval bead

474 **Base-seam template:** Straight Stitch Base Seam 8; **Thread embroidery stitches:** Straight Stitch, Detached Chain Stitch; **Silk ribbon embroidery stitches:** None; **Beads and baubles:** Seed bead, sequin

475 **Base-seam template:** Straight Stitch Base Seam 8; **Thread embroidery stitches:** Straight Stitch, Detached Chain Stitch; **Silk ribbon embroidery stitches:** None; **Beads and baubles:** Seed bead

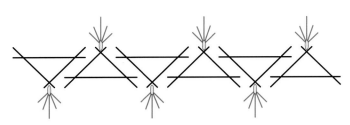

476 **Base-seam template:** Straight Stitch Base Seam 8; **Thread embroidery stitches:** Straight Stitch; **Silk ribbon embroidery stitches:** None; **Beads and baubles:** Rice bead

477 **Base-seam template:** Straight Stitch Base Seam 8; **Thread embroidery stitches:** Straight Stitch, Detached Chain Stitch, French Knot; **Silk ribbon embroidery stitches:** Detached Chain Stitch, Fargo Rose; **Beads and baubles:** None

478 **Base-seam template:** Straight Stitch Base Seam 8; **Thread embroidery stitches:** Straight Stitch, Detached Chain Stitch; **Silk ribbon embroidery stitches:** None; **Beads and baubles:** Seed bead, 2 mm round bead

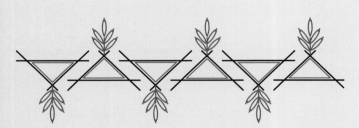

479 **Base-seam template:** Straight Stitch Base Seam 8; **Thread embroidery stitches:** Straight Stitch, Detached Chain Stitch; **Silk ribbon embroidery stitches:** None; **Beads and baubles:** None

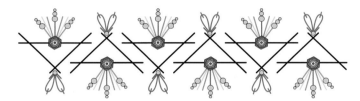

480 **Base-seam template:** Straight Stitch Base Seam 8; **Thread embroidery stitches:** Straight Stitch, Detached Chain Stitch; **Silk ribbon embroidery stitches:** None; **Beads and baubles:** Seed bead, sequin, 2 mm round bead, 3 mm round bead

About the Author

Faith, family, and friends can get you through anything … but stitching will keep you sane!

—*Kathy Seaman Shaw*

Kathy has always shared her knowledge of the needlearts by teaching basic skills in sewing, crocheting, cross-stitch, ribbon embroidery, beading, jewelry making, and traditional quilting at local guilds, women's groups, and the community college in her area.

Her series of free online crazy quilt courses began in 2011 and draws hundreds of ladies from around the globe to her blog annually. Eventually, this interest resulted in the publication of several books for Amazon. This book for C&T Publishing on modern crazy-quilt seam designs begins the next chapter of her creativity.

Crazy quilting allows Kathy to use skills from other hobbies as possible embellishment ideas, keeping creativity flourishing and expanding her knowledge in various techniques. She just can't imagine a more enjoyable creative experience and is happy to share that love of needlearts with anyone who will listen. Kathy is happy to answer questions through her blog, *Shawkl Designs*.

VISIT KATHY ONLINE AND FOLLOW ON SOCIAL MEDIA!

Blog: shawkl.com

Pinterest: /shawkl

Want even more creative content?

Make it, snap it, share it *using* **#ctpublishing**